BUILT NOT BROKEN

RACHEL GAINES

Built Not Broken

ISBN (Paperback): 979-8-9931526-0-8
ISBN (Hardcover): 979-8-9931526-2-2

This is a work of fiction. Names, characters, places, and incidents are either products of the author's imagination or used fictitiously. Any resemblance to actual persons, living or dead, or actual events is purely coincidental.

Cover design: M.Y.T. Morrow
Interior design: M.Y.T. Morrow

Printed in the United States of America

First Edition — September 2025

Published by MYT Morrow Books
Hartwell, Georgia

DEDICATION

For every soul who has
carried silence as a burden.
May your voice rise,
steady and strong.

And to the One who
turns broken things
into new beginnings.

Table of Contents

✦ Act III – The Reckoning

PRELUDE

Millstone

The bus sighed as if it were tired of secrets. Naomi LeBlanc pressed her forehead to the cool glass and watched the highway narrow into a spine of two-lane blacktop. Pines leaned in close as if they meant to hear her thinking. Bridge rails flashed in a stuttering rhythm—silver, shadow, silver—and every mile the air grew thicker, like the land was dissolving into heat and memory.

She had forgotten the smell until it found her again—dust and diesel and something sweet that didn't belong to anything blooming. The kind of scent that clung to your shirt and refused to come out in the wash. The kind that said, in its way: you're almost home, whether you want to be or not.

A baby fussed in the front seat. Its mother rocked with the motion of the road, murmuring a soft rhythm. A teenager three rows back drummed a sneaker heel against the seat, counting a beat only he understood. An old man in a shiny hat, worn across the brim, folded and refolded a newspaper that nobody had asked him to share. Naomi's seatmate, a woman with hands nicked from kitchen work, cradled a paper grocery bag like it was a small animal and turned pecan halves in her palm.

"Storm took down our tree last fall," the woman said finally, with the air of someone who had been rehearsing sentence number one and wasn't sure what to do with number two. "Fifty years of shade. Gone in an afternoon."

"I'm sorry," Naomi said.

"Funny thing," the woman added, rolling a pecan between thumb and forefinger. "After we saw the stump rings, I realized it wasn't as old as I'd made it in my mind. I just got used to telling the same story." She glanced out at the pines and smiled without mirth. "You ever do that? Get used to telling the same story so long you forget to check if it's true?"

Naomi felt the bus seat deepen beneath her, as if the question were a weight she'd put down and then picked back up without meaning to. "Once or twice."

The woman nodded like they'd settled something. "I make two-ingredient biscuits," she said, as if it followed. "Well, two and prayer." She dug into the bag, tore a page from a church bulletin, and wrote in small, neat letters: *self-rising flour + cream*. When she handed the paper over, her ring finger grazed Naomi's knuckles. "You don't look like much of a liar," she said kindly. "Just tired."

Naomi smiled at the paper and slipped it into her tote, where recipes and receipts shared company with a notebook the color of storm water. Tired, yes. The kind of tired that sleep doesn't touch. The kind that sets up house behind your eyes and watches what you watch.

Silence, Millstone's old friend, slid onto the cracked vinyl beside her and crossed its legs as if it had paid for the seat. It had raised her as faithfully as Evelyn had—fed her lessons, pinched her when she forgot them, praised her when she held them steady. *Good girl,* silence would say. *Quiet girl. You won't cause trouble if you don't open your mouth.*

She remembered lessons you could measure—like the three knocks her grandfather drummed on the table when conversation edged too close to the truth. *Stop.* He never said the word; the knocks were enough. And her grandmother's dish rag—wrung twice, folded once, hung just so over the sink—a flag that meant *enough now*. Naomi had learned their signs like other children knew the catechism. Her throat had been her first classroom; swallowing had been her first grade.

Caleb never learned. He laughed with his whole throat and asked questions that weren't invited and looked at men as if he expected to be answered. The memory caught at her mouth—her brother on the back steps, dust on his knees, recounting some detail from shop class like it mattered to the fate of the world. *You can't keep it in and still call it true,* he'd said once, leaning his shoulder into hers. *Truth is not a pet you chain in the yard.*

Naomi pressed her palm to the notebook through the canvas of her bag until the cardboard cover warmed. Some days, she pretended that what she wrote there was Caleb, still talking. Some days she knew better and wrote anyway.

The bus rattled over a bridge harsh enough to shake the windows in their rubber beds. The driver cursed under his breath and patted the dash like a stubborn mule. At the next stop—a gas station hiding behind two live oaks—the driver announced a ten-minute break, and the mother with the baby sighed like she'd been told heaven was only three blocks up and two to the right.

Outside, the heat wrapped itself around Naomi like a wet towel. A boy in cutoffs sprayed a hose across the concrete until a puddle formed, creating a mirror that reflected the sky. The old man with the shiny hat stood bent over the trash can, hand fishing something he insisted he hadn't dropped. Far off, thunder made a sound you felt in your bones more than in your ears. No storm yet. Just promise.

Naomi walked the length of the lot, stretched her back, and leaned on the soda machine to watch the road bend out of sight. She could have kept going. She could have let the bus leave without her and caught another one going in a different direction. Her chest tightened at the thought, which was how she knew she would get back on.

A pickup idled at the pump. Two men in ball caps discussed a man named Joe and a tab that he didn't know how to pay. One said, "He's been talkin' again." The other said, "Bernice is gonna wring him out if she ever gets him home sober." The way they said it told Naomi they knew her people. The way they didn't look at her told her they knew she would know they knew.

A fragment of a hymn came out of the station door when a man opened it—something about being still, something about knowing. Naomi smiled without softness. Millstone loved that verse. It confused quiet for holy and called it obedience.

"Miss," the driver called, palm up in the air like it could gather stragglers. "We're rolling."

She climbed back aboard and took her seat. The pecan woman had fallen asleep with her mouth open just enough to be tender. The teenager's drumbeat had slowed to something like patience. The old man read the same paragraph twice and frowned like the words had emigrated while he wasn't watching.

Naomi put her head against the glass and let the country slide by. Kudzu swallowed whole trees, repairing what it didn't own. A creek flashed once through a break in the brush. A crow regarded the bus from a fence post with a look that said it had time, and she did not. The sky was the color of an old shirt that had been washed too many times.

She drifted into a memory before she could tell herself not to. Eleven years old. August. Evelyn was standing at the sink, wringing that rag, the kitchen smelling of fried eggplant and ironed cotton. Her grandfather knocking once because Aunt Bernice's voice had grown too sharp on Uncle Joe's name. Lydia tapping a pill from a bottle she said was for headaches, but the way her eyes slid away said otherwise. Caleb at the back screen, fingers curled through the mesh, watching the yard like a map to somewhere the adults had forbidden. Naomi felt the memory's old ache move under her ribs, then settle there, a stone she knew how to carry without dropping.

A bump in the road jarred her awake. Ahead, the forest thinned and the land broke open into fields gone to stubble and a water tower with a rusted belly. The bus drew breath and let it go in a slow whine. Then the sign appeared—white letters on wood that should have been replaced, the cheerful lie freshened while the truth beneath it splintered.

WELCOME TO MILLSTONE.

Her throat closed, then opened. It did both things because she had trained it to. The pecan woman startled and blinked at the window. "Home?" she asked, no one in particular.

Naomi LeBlanc didn't answer. Millstone was a place your body knew even when your mind insisted it had forgotten. The church steeple rose first, a white finger sketching at a complicated sky. The diner's roofline hunkered beside it like a friend nobody wanted to be seen with but everybody needed. Porches showed their undersides as the bus rolled past—the ribcage of town life, all those boards, all that watching.

They slowed for a stop sign whose paint had peeled into a topographical map of neglect. At the corner, a boy threw a basketball against a backboard with no net. It made the same hollowness each time. Two little girls clapped their hands and sang about lemonade, and when the bus passed, they stopped mid-rhyme to stare. It was how children learned in Millstone—note what arrived, who stayed, who left, what changed, and what remained the same.

Ruth would say the town hadn't grown a minute since they were kids. Angel would say it had grown meaner. Ruth and Angel. Naomi felt her mouth shape their names, and some of the tightness in her shoulders loosened. Ruth steadied you, fed you, and made you believe that kindness was a muscle, not just a mood. Angel threw her head back when she laughed and aimed her words like stones at windows that needed breaking. They had made promises behind the softball field with a safety pin and chewing gum wrappers. Naomi felt the scar under her thumb where they'd pressed their blood together and vowed to tell the truth even when it made everything harder.

The bus passed the council building—a brick thing that sat too proud for its size. Through the glass doors, Naomi caught a glimpse of a framed photo: a handshake, with a slight smile stretched too wide. Paul's suit always fit like the town had tailored itself around him. She remembered the exact incline of his chin when he said *for the good of the community*, and how her father had once gone quiet in a way that frightened her more than shouting.

Her father had believed in work more than talk. He had believed in moving even when tired. He had said, when she dragged her feet on a summer afternoon, "You rest when you're done, not when you're scared." Naomi had believed him because that's what daughters do with their fathers until the world shows them the complicated footnotes. She still believed him most days. Even on the others, she carried the sentence like a mustard seed in her pocket, rubbing it smooth with worry until it blessed her by accident.

The driver called out names of stops the way a man reads a list he doesn't mind forgetting. "Depot. Main at Court. The Square." A woman rose and then changed her mind and sat back down, shaking her head at a fear that had won one more small argument. The teenager bounded off at Main and didn't look back. The old man in the hat gave his paper to the mother with the baby without being asked and said, "Wrap him in this if the air's too cold." The kindness shocked Naomi so much she had to look out the window again to keep from crying.

They crept past the church—HOPE CHAPEL spelled out on the sign, the white paint bright where a volunteer had refreshed it with a shaky hand. *Be still and know*, the marquee said. *Potluck Sunday*. Naomi's throat warmed with a laugh she didn't let out. Millstone loved potlucks and scriptures that instructed people to hold their tongues.

She watched the steeple with its narrow seams, dry wood set against a summer that forgot rain. It would take only a spark, she thought, and then hated herself for thinking it. Not a wish. Just a knowing of what dried things do.

The bus wheezed into the small lot, the town dignified by calling it a station. Two benches. A corkboard with notices layered so thick that you could peel a decade if you dug your nails just right. A vending machine that offered three candy bars and a stubborn packet of peanuts. In the distance, a dog barked like it had been appointed to keep time.

Naomi's heart did the old trick—stutter, then march. Her body had a memory of leaving here and a fear of returning that didn't measure itself in logic. Somewhere, a cousin would be telling her business in a parking lot. Somewhere, Aunt Bernice would be predicting trouble in a voice that pretended it was prayer. Somewhere, Uncle Joe would be promising a debt would be handled as soon as a man of his word had the money to prove he was one.

Naomi touched the notebook again. She imagined Ruth's hand around a mug, steady as a lighthouse. She imagined Angel's grin like a dare. She imagined Lydia's eyes when the conversation turned toward *don't* and *can't* and *not now*. She imagined Evelyn's dish rag wrung twice, folded once. Enough.

The brakes exhaled. The bus rocked to a gentle halt.

"Millstone," the driver called, his voice too casual for the place it named.

The door folded open with a hiss that always sounded like surrender. Air leaned in. Heat stepped up. The sign on the corkboard waggled slightly in the draft—YARD SALE SATURDAY, BRING CASH.

For a thin slice of a second, Naomi watched the split between inside and out and thought, *I could stay seated.* Thought *I could let the door shut, let the driver check the mirror, let him nod, let us carry on to the end of the line, where Millstone is only a word that other people say.* Thought *I could call Ruth from the next town and tell her I tried.* Thought *I could keep Caleb a memory and not the reason.*

The baby in the front seat laughed—one bubble of sound, pure and unpracticed. It lifted the moment by one inch, just enough to see under it.

Naomi tightened her grip on the strap of her bag until the leather cut a small line into her palm. She breathed in. Not a prayer, not exactly. A sentence she could stand on.

You rest when you're done, not when you're scared.

She didn't rise yet. She let the words settle into her knees, her spine, the hinge of her jaw. She turned her face to the open door and let the heat come to meet her.

"I'm here," she whispered to the space between her and the step. "I'm here."

And then she waited for the smallest beat longer—just enough to feel the town watching—before she stood.

ACT I

A Time of Shadows

CHAPTER 1

Homecoming in Shadows

The bus let Naomi off at the edge of Millstone, as if it were dropping a secret. Gravel crackled under her shoes. Heat pressed against her shoulders, though the sun was lowering, the kind of late light that turned the world to amber and made the dust look holy.

The sign still leaned where it always had—WELCOME TO MILLSTONE—in paint that someone had tried to refresh without fixing the wood beneath. That was the town in a sentence: new paint on rot.

Naomi took a breath that stung and tasted like tin. The air smelled the way memory does—sweet in places, sour where it shouldn't be. She adjusted the strap of her tote, felt the grit under her fingers, and started walking.

Silence fell in step beside her—Millstone's oldest companion. As a girl, she'd learned its weight the way other kids learned piano or softball: hours of practice, correction when she slipped, the praise that came when she held it perfectly. Good girl. Quiet girl. The kind who kept a story inside until it curdled.

She passed the diner first, as you always do. The bell over the door had a pitch you could pick out of a thunderstorm. Through the window, Loretta's hair was piled halfway to God, and three men in seed caps leaned over coffee like it might confess. Loretta's eyes flicked up as if they were attached to a tripwire and found Naomi on the sidewalk. One beat. Two. Loretta's mouth made a soft O, then flattened into a line that could have been welcome or a warning.

Naomi kept walking. The church came next, brick-freckled and familiar, with the white sign out front offering a verse and a smiley face. BE STILL AND KNOW, it said, and beneath that: POTLUCK THIS SUNDAY. She almost laughed. Being still had never meant quiet around here; it meant behaving.

Her mother's porch looked smaller than it had in her childhood. The steps complained the way old bones do when she climbed them, the handrail smooth where hands had learned to grip and not fall. The front door was painted the same soft green Evelyn loved, the color of the mint sprigs she'd float in tea when company came.

Naomi stood for a moment, pressing her palm flat against the wood. She could see her reflection in the small rectangle of glass at the top—tired, older than she'd planned to look by now, hair pulled back in a way that kept the world from seeing it shake.

The lock clicked. The door opened. Evelyn stood there with a dish towel in her hands, like a flag she wasn't sure how to wave.

"You came," Evelyn said, and she didn't sound surprised, but she also didn't sound relieved.

"You knew I would," Naomi said.

Inside, the air smelled like lemon polish and fried okra, like Sunday and summer and staying in line. The house wasn't big, but when Naomi was small, it had seemed to hold every piece of the world that mattered. Her father's chair still lived under the window. The afghan Naomi's grandmother crocheted was draped in the exact same diagonal. Even the soft dent in the couch cushion had not forgiven time.

"You hungry?" Evelyn asked, because sometimes a question is a tourniquet.

"I ate on the bus," Naomi lied.

Evelyn nodded, folding the dishtowel once, then twice, as if it had done something to her. "Your sister called," she said. "She said if you stopped by, to stop by." The corner of Evelyn's mouth twitched. "You know how she is."

"I do," Naomi said, and the ache that Lydia's name carried surprised her.

They stood there, two women with the same eyes and different spines, the distance between them set with invisible furniture—things they never put down, things they never named. Naomi let the quiet sit as long as she could bear it and then moved past her mother into the kitchen.

"Tea?" Evelyn asked, already reaching for the kettle.

"Please," Naomi said, because there are rituals you honor even when you're angry.

Evelyn's hands were quick, practiced. Steam lifted. The comfort should have come with it, but it didn't. Naomi watched the way her mother's knuckles whitened around the handle and was ten years old again, sitting at this table while the adults talked in half-sentences and made a mountain out of a whisper.

She felt it coming—the warning, the plea, the dressed-up fear. It lived in the fine lines at the corners of Evelyn's mouth. It rattled the teaspoon.

"Naomi." Evelyn didn't look up. "Whatever you think you're here to do—just remember where you are."

"I know exactly where I am," Naomi said. "That's why I came."

Evelyn set the cups down, saucers clicking lightly. She sat. Her posture was a sermon on its own—chin lifted, shoulders back, the spine that got her through years of not being allowed to break.

"You've stirred things up," Evelyn said.

"Things needed stirring."

"Paul says—"

"Paul always says," Naomi said without meaning to, the words sharper than she wanted to throw.

Silence, again. Only the clock over the stove dared speak. Naomi watched the seconds tick by and wished they would pass more quickly.

Evelyn tried a new door. "Ruth and Angel were by yesterday," she said. "Ruth brought over a casserole. Angel brought over opinions."

That pulled a smile from Naomi. "That sounds exactly right."

"They're good girls," Evelyn said. "They always have been."

"They're women," Naomi said softly. "And they're mine."

Evelyn's mouth pressed thin. "Don't make this about lines in the sand," she said. "This is home."

Naomi let the word lie there. Home. It felt like a coat she used to wear that no longer fit in the arms. "I'm not the one who turned it into a line," she said. "I'm just the one who stopped stepping over it."

Evelyn looked at her daughter—the set of her jaw, the tiredness in her eyes—and something wavered. She reached as if she might touch Naomi's hand, then let her fingers find the saucer instead. "Eat something," she said, because she had to say something, because she did not yet have the words for "I'm sorry," or "I was wrong," or "I'm afraid for you."

"I will," Naomi said, and stood. "After I see Ruth."

Ruth's house had always been a place the town couldn't quite penetrate. The hydrangeas knew how to bloom without asking permission. The porch swing still sang the same soft note when you set it going. Ruth opened the door before Naomi's knuckles found it, pulled her into a hug that smelled like flour and lavender and Sundays that didn't hurt.

"There you are," Ruth said, holding Naomi's face in her hands as if she could keep it from slipping into whatever Millstone had planned. "You look like you slept on a bus."

"I did."

"Then I'll pretend I didn't see it and feed you anyway."

Naomi let herself be ushered into the kitchen, where everything had its place and every place was clean. A pie cooled on the counter—peach, by the look and the mercy in the air. Angel sat on the table's edge, swinging her legs, hair braided back tight, eyes bright the way danger is.

"Look what the cat dragged back," Angel said, but her smile was all relief. She hopped down and hugged Naomi until Naomi could finally breathe again.

"You're late," Angel added.

"I'm here," Naomi said.

They ate pie hot enough to hurt a little and drank coffee that forgave them for it. Ruth asked questions that were really caring—how was the trip, did Evelyn fuss, did the house feel the same—and Naomi took each one like a sip, grateful for something that went down without clawing.

Angel didn't bother with the small talk for long. "So what's the plan?" she asked, fork tapping the plate. "Because you didn't come back to sit quietly and cross-stitch."

"Angel," Ruth said gently.

"What? She didn't." Angel turned to Naomi. "You gonna call him out? You gonna go to the council? You gonna light a match?"

Naomi pushed a peach around with her fork. "I'm going to start with telling the truth out loud," she said. "And see who tries to shut the door on it."

"Paul will," Angel said. "He was born shutting doors."

Ruth sighed. "It's not just him. It's the ones who let him. The ones who think keeping the peace is the same as keeping each other."

Naomi looked down at her hands. There were a few white lines across her knuckles—faint scars that didn't have good stories, just true ones. "I'm tired," she said. "But tired isn't the same as done."

Ruth smiled, pleased at the shape of that sentence. "No, it isn't."

Angel leaned in, elbows on the table. "You remember when we were twelve and we signed a blood pact behind the softball field?"

Ruth wrinkled her nose. "We did not."

"We did," Angel said, delighted. "We pricked our thumbs with that terrible safety pin Naomi stole from her mama's sewing box and promised to tell each other the truth even when it hurt."

Ruth shook her head, but her eyes were soft. "I remember promising," she said. "I don't recall the blood."

"Oh, there was blood," Angel said. "I nearly fainted."

Naomi laughed, sudden and easy, the sound surprising her. "We meant it," she said. "We still do."

"Then we start," Angel said, serious again. "You won't do this alone."

Ruth set her mug down with that careful precision she gave to everything that mattered. "You can stay here," she said. "If things... if the town..." She didn't finish, because she didn't need to.

"I have a room at Mama's," Naomi said.

Ruth made a face that said she knew what that meant. "Then at least don't walk home in the dark."

Angel stood. "Better yet, don't walk home at all. I'll drive you."

"You don't have a car," Naomi said.

"I'll steal one," Angel said, and the grin she threw cut the heaviness in the room in half.

They drove anyway—Ruth insisted—and circled the blocks the way you do when you want a thing to know you see it. Millstone was both smaller and bigger than Naomi remembered: smaller in the way every street had been walked a hundred times and thus belonged to her feet, bigger in the way secrets had grown in the cracks between the boards.

They passed Lydia's duplex. A lamp was on, the shade crooked. Naomi wanted to go in, but she also wanted to wait until she wasn't holding so many trembling things.

"Tomorrow," Ruth said, reading her friend without being told.

"Tomorrow," Naomi agreed.

At the corner of Oak and Third, an old man in a folding chair tipped his cap. He'd watched every year of Naomi's childhood from that spot, counting cars like blessings. Two teenage boys on bikes cut too close, and Angel leaned out the window just enough to make them laugh and swerve.

They slowed by the council building. The brick looked newer than the church's, the windows smug. Through the glass, Naomi could see a framed photo of Paul shaking hands with a state senator, both of them wearing the smile men wear when they're thinking about the smell of their own cologne.

"Don't stare at him," Ruth said. "Make him stare at you."

Naomi didn't know if she had that kind of light yet, but she wanted it.

By the time they pulled back in front of Evelyn's, the porch light was on. Fireflies stitched the yard in lazy, bright threads. Naomi got out, and the night washed over her, a bowl of sound—the cicadas, the dog three doors down, someone's screen door complaining.

Ruth put the car in park. "Call if you need," she said. "Call if you don't."

Angel leaned across Ruth and pointed a finger, a gesture both blessing and daring. "Don't let silence sit next to you," she said. "If it climbs on the couch, push it off."

Naomi nodded, the corner of her mouth lifting. "Yes, ma'am."

She went up the steps slower than she'd come down them earlier. Inside, Evelyn had left a plate of cornbread wrapped in a towel. Naomi unwrapped it, tore a piece with her fingers, and ate standing at the counter. It tasted like everything she loved and everything she resented.

She carried her bag to her old room. The bedspread had been replaced, but the dent in the carpet where her desk had been was still pressed into the fibers. On the bookshelf, a cracked-spine copy of *To Kill a Mockingbird* leaned against a stack of church programs bound with a rubber band that had gone brittle.

Naomi set her tote on the bed and pulled out the little notebook she always traveled with. The first page was an old recipe she'd jotted down from a woman on the bus who swore she could make biscuits with two ingredients and prayer. The second page was blank. She clicked her pen and wrote Caleb at the top in careful letters. She didn't write anything beneath it for a long time. The name was a whole paragraph by itself.

When she finally put the pen down, her hand cramped. She flexed it, stared at the ceiling, and listened to the house settle. In the hallway, Evelyn's footsteps paused outside Naomi's door. The shadow at the crack was a thin line, there and then gone.

Naomi turned off the lamp and lay back. The ceiling fan pushed the warm air around like a rumor. She closed her eyes, and the town did not.

She could feel Millstone thinking. She could feel it counting. She could feel it deciding who to be with her at home again.

"Move even when you're tired," her father used to say when summer chores had stretched too long and she had tried to bargain for shade. "You rest when you're done, not when you're scared."

Naomi let the words fill the room, just as water finds every low place. She didn't know if she believed them tonight, but she let them stand guard.

Somewhere, far off, a bell struck the hour. She rolled to her side and pulled the sheet to her chin. The tiredness that lived in her bones wasn't going away by morning, she knew. But morning was coming anyway.

And when it did, she would be in it.

She would not be quiet.

She would move.

CHAPTER 2

Echoes of the Past

Morning came in strips through the blinds, laying thin ladders of light across Naomi's floor. The house made its old sounds—pipes clearing their throats, a cupboard clicking shut two rooms away, Evelyn's careful steps rehearsing the path from stove to sink. Naomi lay awake long enough to memorize the rhythm and then got up before it could settle into her.

She washed her face at the bathroom sink with water that ran warm, then cold. In the mirror, her eyes looked like her father's on early workdays: stubborn and not ready. She tied her hair back, slid on the same shoes she'd worn off the bus, and met Evelyn in the kitchen.

"I made grits," Evelyn said, as if declaring a truce. "And scrambled eggs. Toast if you want it."

"Thank you," Naomi said. She sat. The plate was too full, the way mothers plate food when they're trying to fix something they can't name. Naomi ate what she could and let the rest go cold.

Evelyn hovered with the coffee pot. "I'm going into town later," she said. "Need anything?"

"No," Naomi said. "I thought I'd walk."

Evelyn swallowed. "All right." The word meant I can't stop you. It also meant I wish I could.

When Naomi reached the door, Evelyn spoke to the window over the sink. "If people say things," she said, "don't hold it like it's yours."

Naomi stood on the porch and let the screen door sigh behind her. "I'll try," she said, and stepped into the day.

The diner breathed coffee and bacon grease and old stories. Loretta's hair was stacked higher than yesterday—as if she'd added a ring for each rumor that passed through. The bell rang out when Naomi pushed the door open and then announced her presence to the room in a pitch that made heads turn.

Three seconds of quiet lay over everything like a cloth, and then spoons clinked again, the low hum resuming with a new note threaded in. Naomi slipped onto a stool at the counter. The vinyl stuck to the back of her knees.

"Morning," Loretta said, too bright, already pouring. "You look like a biscuit girl today. You want a biscuit?"

"I want two," Naomi said.

A smile tugged at Loretta's mouth—the first honest thing in the room. "Two it is."

At the far booth, a woman from the church—Sister May with the strong perfume and stronger opinions—whispered too loud to be accidental. "She's got a lot of nerve, showing her face like she's not the reason folks are upset."

"Nobody's upset," the man across from her said, and then added, "out loud," like he wished he could reel it back.

"People are fine until somebody starts trouble," Sister May replied, eyes cutting toward Naomi's back. "Then everybody remembers what should have stayed forgotten."

Loretta set the coffee down and leaned in just enough for Naomi to hear. "You want my apron? I can make a scene if you need me to."

Naomi blew on the coffee. "No scenes. Not yet."

The door opened—Ruth's steady step, Angel's faster one. They brought air in with them, the way some people do. Angel took the stool on Naomi's right and drummed her fingers on the counter. Ruth slid onto the left and folded her hands in prayer.

"Morning," Ruth said. "Loretta, if you give us that corner booth later, I'll write you into my will."

"You already tried that," Loretta said. "All you left me was a pie dish and a fern."

"She's a lying woman," Angel told Naomi. "She left me nothing."

"Because you killed the fern," Ruth said. Then, to Naomi, low: "How's your spirit?"

"Upright," Naomi said. "Shaky in the knees."

Angel glanced toward Sister May's booth and pitched her voice just high enough. "Isn't it a beautiful day to mind your own business?"

Sister May's mouth opened and closed, a fish catching air. She turned her shoulder deliberately. Ruth set a forearm across Angel's tapping hand without looking.

The bell chimed again. Deacon Whitlow heaved himself onto a stool three down from Naomi, a man built like an oak stump and about as flexible. He removed his cap as if someone were watching for the gesture. "Mornin'," he boomed, politeness that came with an edge.

Loretta poured him coffee without being asked. He didn't drink it yet—he aimed it like an object lesson. "Miss Naomi," he said finally, as if he were granting permission. "Heard you were back. Heard you've been busy."

"I've been truthful," Naomi said.

"Truth," he repeated, rolling the word around like a pebble. "Truth without wisdom can be a hammer in the hands of a child."

Angel looked delighted. "Good thing she's not a child."

Ruth made a sound that could have been a sigh or a warning. Deacon Whitlow turned to Ruth. "You'd do well to keep your friend from makin' messes she can't clean."

Ruth's face didn't change, but something in her gaze sharpened. "We've been cleaning messes made by men since before you learned to hold a broom, Deacon."

A few heads popped up. Loretta coughed into a napkin, badly hiding a smile. Sister May's eyes gleamed.

Deacon Whitlow set his cap on the counter, slow and careful. "This town's got a way of doin' things," he said, voice dropping. "Always has. Folks who forget that tend to regret the rememberin' they chase."

Naomi felt the old urge to swallow words whole and save herself the burn. Her father's voice rose up, steady as a fencepost: You rest when you're done, not when you're scared. She set her coffee down.

"I know the way this town does things," Naomi said, evenly. "It does them quiet. It calls peace. But it's only quiet for the ones who benefit from the hush."

Deacon Whitlow's lip twitched. "A body could call that slander."

"A body could call it Sunday," Angel muttered. Ruth pressed her knee against Angel's under the counter—a nudge, not a muzzle.

"Breakfast is ready," Loretta cut in, saving everyone. She slid plates toward Naomi, Ruth, and Angel. "Deacon, you want your usual or you want to sit there and chew the air?"

He grunted. "Usual."

They ate. Naomi's hands steadied with every bite, the biscuit breaking clean, butter shining. The room's hum shifted—still charged, but less like a storm and more like humidity you learn to live in. When Ruth finished, she squeezed Naomi's forearm.

"Lydia?" Ruth asked.

"After this," Naomi said.

Angel wiped her mouth and set the napkin down like a flag. "I'll drive you."

"You don't have a car," Ruth and Naomi said together.

"I will manifest one," Angel said, and Loretta laughed so hard she had to lean on the coffee pot.

Lydia's duplex smelled like last night and the night before—coffee left too long on the heat, lemon cleaner, a sweetness undercut by the bite of pills. She opened the door with her hair back and her eyes edged in red.

"You look good," Naomi said.

"You look like a lie," Lydia said, and then she pulled Naomi into a hug that surprised them both.

The living room had sagging furniture, an afghan that had traveled through three houses, and a picture of Caleb tucked in the corner of the mirror as if the glass could hold him. Lydia followed Naomi's gaze and flinched.

"I meant to take that down," she said. "It keeps startling me."

"Maybe it should," Naomi said, gently.

Lydia moved through the room with a restlessness that made Naomi's teeth ache. She picked up a stack of mail, set it down, rearranged a magazine, and found a pill bottle with her fingers without looking. Then, she seemed to realize Naomi was watching.

"I'm fine," Lydia said.

"I didn't ask if you were fine," Naomi said.

"Good," Lydia said. "Because I'm not."

She sat. Naomi took the couch opposite and sank a little too far. The springs complained. Outside, a kid passed on a scooter, the wheels squealing as they hit the seam in the sidewalk.

"I saw Mama this morning," Naomi said.

"I know," Lydia said. "She called me after you left and told me she made too much breakfast."

"She always does when she's worried," Naomi said.

"She always is," Lydia replied.

They looked at each other across a coffee table covered in ring marks. Naomi chose her words the way she chose steps on creek stones. "I'm not going to stop," she said. "You know that."

Lydia's mouth twisted. "I know it like I know I should take my medicine with food." She rubbed the heel of her hand against her temple. "Naomi, they are going to make you pay for every word."

"I already paid for the quiet," Naomi said. "I'm tired of that bill."

Lydia stared at Caleb's photo again. He was captured mid-laugh, eyes crinkled, mouth open like he was about to say something he never got to finish. "I keep dreaming he's at the door," she said. "He knocks and knocks and I open it and it's just… it's that boy from down the street trying to sell me magazine subscriptions." She laughed, a ragged sound. "And I'm relieved and furious both."

Naomi reached across and squeezed Lydia's hand. "You don't have to tell me anything today," she said. "We can sit. Or we can walk. Or we can go to Ruth's and let her feed us like birds."

Lydia's mouth softened. "She will too," she said. "She'll put pie in my hand like I'm a child."

"You are many things," Naomi said. "Child is rarely one."

Lydia leaned back. "Aunt Bernice called last night," she said, voice flattening. "Said Uncle Joe's been talkin' in the bar again. Said if you keep pokin' around, the wrong man's going to remember who owes who."

The words set a cold down Naomi's spine. Uncle Joe had a way of making his own trouble and renting it out. "Did Bernice say who he was owing this time?"

Lydia shook her head. "Said he kept calling it 'old debt' like that made it noble."

Naomi let the new thread sit with the others. Millstone's quilt of secrets was pieced from so many hands.

"Come to the diner with me tomorrow," Naomi said. "Sit with me where everybody can see us. Let them remember you're not a ghost."

"I feel like one," Lydia said.

"Then let them see you haunt," Angel's voice said from the doorway. She'd slipped in quietly, leaning against the frame with a grin. "Sorry," she added, not sorry at all. "Door was open. Also, your neighbor says hello, and she's making brownies that are a spiritual experience."

Lydia laughed, a sound that loosened something in the room. "That woman cannot bake a cookie to save her life."

"She said brownies, not cookies," Angel said. "Don't slander a woman who brings offerings."

Naomi stood. "Walk with us," she said. "Just around the block."

Lydia hesitated, then grabbed a sweatshirt, despite the warmth. "Fine," she said. "But if Sister May drives by, I'm hiding behind the hydrangeas."

"Join the club," Angel said.

They walked the block slowly. The sun had climbed, and the street broke into pockets of shade. On one porch, a grandfather shelling beans glanced up and then down like he hadn't. Two little girls played hand games on the steps and sang about lemonade. They fell silent when the women passed, and then, after a beat, picked the song back up but softer.

"See?" Angel said. "Haunting works."

Naomi felt eyes on her from places she couldn't point to—slats in blinds, the sliver between curtain and frame, the gap in a screen door. She didn't quicken her step. She let her shoulders stay level. You rest when you're done, she told her bones. Not when you're watched.

When they looped back to Lydia's, a pickup rolled past slowly. The driver—one of Paul's men—kept his face forward, but the mirror tilt said enough. Angel lifted two fingers off her hip in a salute that wasn't polite. The truck didn't speed up. It just kept going, like a promise.

"I hate this," Lydia said. "I hate that my street feels like a test."

"It is," Naomi said. "But we'll cheat. We'll look at each other's papers."

Lydia cracked a smile. "Go," she said. "Before Mama starts calling both our phones and then walks over with a casserole like an excuse."

"She will," Naomi said.

"She will," Lydia echoed, love tucked into the sigh.

Naomi cut back toward the square alone. The council building threw its clean shadow across the sidewalk. She paused across from it, her heart ticking steadily and fast. Through the glass, a poster announced a "Community Listening Session" in two days. The word listening felt like a dare.

"You're early," a voice said.

Naomi turned. Brother Harlan—one of the quieter elders—stood by the newspaper box, hands in his pockets, face pinched from years of polite swallowing.

"Early for what?" Naomi asked.

"For whatever storm you brought with you," he said. No malice in it. Maybe something like hope, thin, and shy.

"I didn't bring it," Naomi said. "I just stopped pretending it wasn't there."

He nodded, the smallest thing. "Sometimes that's all it takes." He left her with that, went inside for a paper he might not read, and Naomi watched the door swing shut on his back.

On her way to Evelyn's, she cut past her grandparents' old place—a shotgun house with peeling paint and a chain-link fence that never once kept a secret in. She could still see her grandfather's hand on the arm of his chair, the way he'd tap it when someone said too much, the family's sign for that's far enough. Her grandmother had her own sign: a dishrag wrung twice and hung just so. Naomi paused at the gate and touched the cold metal. "No more," she whispered to the porch that knew the shape of that rag. "Not in my mouth."

By the time she reached the green door, her legs ached in the good way. Evelyn was at the table with a stack of envelopes and a pen, writing her name on bills so that she could keep them from being late.

"How's your sister?" Evelyn asked, not looking up.

"Breathing," Naomi said. "Walking with us tomorrow. Maybe eating brownies."

"She never could stand that neighbor's baking," Evelyn said, and relief spread across her face like warmth.

Naomi poured water and drank half the glass before she remembered she was thirsty. "There's a meeting," she said. "In two days. They called it listening."

Evelyn's pen stopped. "Are you going?"

"I'm not behind anymore," Naomi said, and felt how true it was in her throat. "I'm where I'm supposed to be."

Evelyn set the pen down and folded her hands. It took her a long time to lift her eyes, and when she did, they were wet. "Then I'll buy a new dress," she said. "The kind you wear when you stand up."

Naomi smiled, small and sure. Outside, a truck rolled by without slowing. The house breathed. The town tilted. And for the first time since stepping off the bus, Naomi felt the day catch up with her, not to push her down, but to push her forward.

CHAPTER
3

*Small Town,
Sharp Tongues*

Naomi woke before the alarm, the house already alive with the soft choreography of Evelyn's morning—water running, cupboard hinges clicking, a chair leg scraping the linoleum, and then being nudged back into place. She lay still and listened. It was the same music she'd grown up to, the same rhythm that had taught her how to time her breath to other people's comfort. Today she matched it for a moment, then deliberately broke time—swinging her legs over the side of the bed and planting her feet on the rug while the house was still mid-inhale.

Outside, the early light had not yet burned the dew off the grass. A lawnmower coughed two streets over, and a dog aired its opinion about a squirrel that knew the fence's exact limits. Naomi washed her face, tied her hair, and stepped into the hall. Evelyn glanced up from the table where she was addressing envelopes—careful handwriting, a row of stamps fanned like a patient hand of cards.

"I made oatmeal," Evelyn said. "And toast. If you'd rather grits, I can—"

"Oatmeal is good," Naomi said. She sat and let her mother set the bowl down with the same practiced gentleness she'd used when Naomi was six. The spoon clinked against the rim. Naomi tried to swallow the first bite around a knot that had nothing to do with oats.

Evelyn topped off Naomi's glass with water and pretended to fuss with the napkin holder. "You walking again?"

"I like the air," Naomi said, and let it be the truth it was.

Evelyn's eyes flicked to the window. "If people say things," she began, and then, catching herself, changed the sentence mid-air. "If you need a ride, call Ruth. Or Angel. Or… me."

Naomi nodded. The thread of something new in Evelyn's voice—permission, maybe; resignation, maybe—warmed the back of her neck. "I'm going to stop by the diner. Then Lydia's."

"Tell her to eat something," Evelyn said automatically, and the practiced line carried so many unsaid things Naomi felt the whole house tilt.

She finished the oatmeal, kissed her mother's temple, and stepped out. The porch boards complained in a familiar way beneath her weight, an old language she still understood: We've carried you before. We can carry you again.

The air smelled like a promise and a dare.

At the diner, the bell sang its thin metal note, the one you could pick out from three blocks away. Morning regulars had already indentured themselves to coffee; hats were tipped back, boots braced against the foot rail. The fan turned slowly, moving warm air from one place to another as if that counted as mercy.

"Look at you, early bird," Loretta said, doing a slow spin with a pot in her hand, lipstick a shade that would outlive all of them. "Well, if it isn't Naomi LeBlanc. You want coffee like a sinner or tea like a saint?"

"Coffee," Naomi said. "Make it a baptism."

"That I can do." Loretta poured, then set a biscuit on a plate with the precision of a communion wafer. "And manna."

Naomi smiled. The smell of butter rose and undid three knots at once.

Down the counter, Frank Bentlee hunched over a newspaper he never bought, his forearms the color of permanent sun. He didn't lift his head when he said, "Girl comes back, thinks she's the prophet we ordered," but the sound carried. A few eyes lifted from their eggs; one mouth twitched toward a grin, but then thought better.

Before Naomi could answer—if she would have—Ruth slid onto the stool at her left, smooth as a hymn. Angel took the right like a cymbal crash, braid swinging, eyes bright with mischief that could turn righteous without warning.

"You order for us because you love us," Angel told Naomi, and then to Loretta, "And make mine with the bacon that you hide from the weak."

"I hide nothing," Loretta said. "I simply don't advertise what the Lord intended."

Ruth rested her forearms on the counter and leaned into Naomi's shoulder. "You good?"

"Standing," Naomi said. "Which is more than some folks want."

"That's right," Angel said, flipping her braid like an exclamation point. "Feet planted, jaw set, hands ready. I brought my good mouth today."

"Leave your bad one in the car," Ruth murmured.

Frank rustled his paper loudly, which is the sound a certain kind of man makes instead of names. "Joe was at Murphy's again," he said toward the sports section. "Talking big about old debts and new men."

Angel's attention snapped like a rubber band. "Your Uncle Joe or the other one who owes everybody and prays about it later?"

"Mine," Naomi said, feeling heat creep under her skin.

Frank pretended not to listen to himself. "Bernice called Murphy at closing. Said to tell Joe to get his hide home before she locks him out and sells his boots."

Loretta snorted. "I'd pay to watch Bernice sell those boots while he's still in them."

Ruth shot Naomi a look: Are you all right? Naomi lifted one shoulder: I'm fine and I'm not.

"Folks are saying Paul's covered tabs before," another man at the corner said without turning. "Ain't a gift, though. He keeps receipts even on what he doesn't write down."

Angel's jaw tightened. "Like a man who thinks the town is his ledger."

Ruth's hand found Naomi's and squeezed once. "Eat," she said softly. "You can't fight a ledger on an empty stomach."

Naomi tore the biscuit in half. Steam curled up, buttery and honest. She took a bite, chewed, swallowed. The small, ordinary act steadied her more than she wanted to admit.

On cue, Sister May swept in, half her perfume arriving a breath ahead. She chose a booth twenty feet from Naomi and angled herself so her profile caught the light. Two church women slid in opposite her, their purses forming a bunched fence along the seat.

"I am not one to traffic in foolishness," Sister May declared, opening a napkin like a map. "But I tell you the Lord is not pleased with chaos."

One of the women made sympathetic teeth. "Mmm."

"And some people don't know the difference between truth and trouble."

"Mmm," the other echoed, both syllables sharp.

Angel flashed a grin. "If they say one more 'mmm,' I'm going to start a choir."

"Angel," Ruth warned gently.

Naomi set her coffee down. "Let them sing," she said, softly. "We'll sing louder when it matters."

Loretta slid plates their way. "Here." She leaned across the counter and looked Naomi in the face the way a person does when she intends to say something that can't be misheard. "You know grit isn't screaming, baby," she said. "It's the way you come back tomorrow."

Naomi nodded, throat tight. "I'll be here."

"Then eat your eggs."

They did. While they ate, the room arranged itself back around them, as rooms will, until the tension felt like humidity instead of thunder.

When they were done, the three women moved from the counter to a small table by the window. The light made halos of floating dust. Outside, Mr. Greer watered his petunias with studied indifference to the fact that he was aiming as much at the sidewalk as the flowers. A boy in a football jersey practiced jukes between parking meters, his breath puffing little ghosts in the warming air.

"I need to see Lydia," Naomi said.

"We'll go with you," Ruth said.

Angel made a face. "Or I could go on ahead and tackle anybody who looks sideways."

"You don't own a car," Ruth reminded.

"I can borrow one from the Lord," Angel said. "He knows my heart."

They stood to leave. Sister May's gaze followed them to the door, bright with a righteousness that bit the skin. Outside, the bell gave its farewell chirp, and the street swallowed them.

Lydia's duplex sat a block off the square, painted beige as a surrender flag. Today, the blinds were open a sliver, which Naomi decided to take as a good sign. Lydia answered in a sweatshirt, though the day was warming, hair clipped up with the kind of care that says I tried, at least.

"You look better," Naomi said.

"You look like a person who lies kindly," Lydia replied, but she softened it with a hug that went on longer than sarcasm would allow. She stepped aside and pulled them into the living room. "I have made coffee that tastes like penance. Who wants in?"

Angel lifted both hands. "Baptize me twice."

Ruth took the mugs from Lydia's shaking fingers and distributed them without comment. Naomi sat on the couch and sank until the springs complained. On the mirror above the console, Caleb's photo was tucked into the frame. Every time Naomi saw it, her breath hit the same rock.

Lydia saw her watching. "I keep meaning to put that away," she said. "And then I don't. It's like a splinter I'm not ready to pull."

Naomi stood and straightened the corner of the picture. "Or a compass," she said.

Lydia made a slight sound, half laugh, half sob, and then, like she'd decided to run while her legs still remembered how, she spoke fast. "Bernice called last night," she said. "Said Joe was at Murphy's spitting history at anybody with ears. Said if you start waving papers, Naomi, certain people will stop paying for his beer and start charging for his breath."

Angel leaned forward. "I hate that man a little bit."

"We don't hate family," Ruth said, automatically, then sighed. "We pray for them, and then sometimes we tell them to hush."

"We've done a lot of the second," Naomi said.

Lydia went to the window and peeked out the slat. "Two of Paul's men were across the street around midnight," she said. "Smoking and laughing like humor was a weapon."

Ruth went still. "Did they knock?"

"No," Lydia said. "They just existed loudly."

Angel stood. "I'll exist louder."

"Angel," Ruth said again, but softer. "We will be loud in the right places."

Lydia rubbed her forearm as if words might be written there and she could smear them away. "I can't decide if I want you to burn it down or go to sleep," she told Naomi. "Both sound like mercy."

"I'm not building churches to burn them," Naomi said. "I'm opening windows."

"That's how you burn a house around here," Lydia said, but she smiled without teeth, so Naomi took it as permission to stay.

They sat a while longer, the four of them letting the coffee cool in their hands, as if they were warming something small and shivering. When they left, Ruth kissed Lydia's cheek. Angel squeezed her shoulder. Naomi pressed her palm to the doorframe as she stepped out, a habit she had when she wanted a place to know she knew it mattered.

Outside, the heat had begun to take hold of the day. Two teenage cousins—Micah and Tess, Aunt Bernice's kids—breezed down the sidewalk with the kind of confidence you wear when you're practicing being grown. Micah nodded once at Naomi, then looked away too quickly. Tess's mouth twisted—familiar family shape. She glanced back, then forward, then back again.

"Tell your mama I'll bring the casserole dish by," Naomi called gently.

Tess's chin lifted an inch. "She said you should drop it on the porch."

Angel made a delighted noise. "I love a porch drama."

Micah elbowed his sister. "We gotta go," he muttered, and they hurried off. Naomi watched the way their shoulders touched even when they weren't trying. Children carry the house with them until they build their own.

"You want to talk to Bernice?" Ruth asked.

"Not until my mouth can do it without breaking," Naomi said.

"Fair."

They cut across the square toward the grocery. The council building stood in its clean brick certainty, catching sunlight like a beacon. Through the glass, a poster advertised a COMMUNITY LISTENING SESSION in two days—the word *'listening' curled at the edges like paper left in the* rain.

Brother Harlan—quiet backbone under a soft jacket—pushed out the door as they approached. He nodded to Ruth, then to Angel, and last to Naomi, with something like apology and hope layered together.

"You coming to the session?" Naomi asked.

"Always did have ears," he said. "Just trying to use them for once." He tipped his chin at the poster. "We'll see if they do."

Inside the grocery, the air-conditioning blessed them. Naomi walked slowly through the produce aisle, a child again beside her mother, taught to pick up a peach as if it could bruise from a glance. She chose three, then put one back—small economies of care. Ruth inspected tomatoes with priestly attention. Angel tried free grapes like a teen and then bought the bag because guilt was her love language.

Halfway to the register, Aunt Bernice materialized at the end of an aisle—lipstick neat, hair set, a cart that announced competence. Her eyes, when they landed on Naomi, did a quick calculation and then settled into something that wanted to pass for affection and couldn't quite.

"Naomi," Bernice said. "You back?"

"I am," Naomi said. "How's Uncle Joe?"

Bernice's mouth compressed. "You know how he is."

"I do," Naomi said gently. "Is he... safe?"

"He's breathing," Bernice said, which in Millstone meant that was all she could promise. She moved closer, lowered her voice. "Baby, you stir in old pots, you wake ghosts. Some of 'em got hands."

Naomi matched her tone. "Some of 'em are already awake. They've been waking me for years."

Bernice's eyes flicked toward Ruth and Angel, who had politely pretended to be considering cereal. "You say Paul's name out loud, that man doesn't just hear it. He hears who said it. And he doesn't forget who eats his bread." She smoothed a hand down her blouse, gathering herself. "You bring that dish by around five," she added in a normal voice, as if the last thirty seconds hadn't happened. "I'll be home."

"Okay," Naomi said. When Bernice moved on, Naomi let her shoulders fall a fraction. The small exchanges—these were the ones that wore a person thin. Not the threats. The care was dressed in caution. The love boiled down to silence.

They paid and stepped back into the heat that had grown bold. A church bell somewhere marked the half hour with an authority Naomi wanted to steal and use differently. As they crossed in front of Hope Chapel, Sister May emerged with two women in tow, voices pitched at the exact register where gossip calls itself prayer.

"…and we will lay hands on it," Sister May declared, "because confusion is not from God."

Ruth stopped, smiling like a blade. "Sister May," she said warmly. "Confusion isn't, no. Control isn't either."

Sister May blinked. "We are praying for unity," she said, adjusting her grip on her purse as if she were shifting theology.

"Pray for courage," Ruth said sweetly. "Unity will come along if it's meant to."

Angel coughed, just once, in a way that sounded suspiciously like *amen*. They moved on before the second volley could launch.

By the time Naomi reached Evelyn's, the weight of small things had stacked—Loretta's biscuit pressed into her palm, Micah's glance away, Bernice's warning, the grocery store hum, the bell's insistence, the word *listening* on clean paper. None of it was a showdown. All of it was a battle.

Evelyn was shelling peas at the table, fingers moving like a piano player's when the hymn is one she's known since childhood. She didn't look up when Naomi came in; she just reached into the bowl and shook a handful of greens into the colander.

"How's Lydia?" Evelyn asked.

"Trying," Naomi said. "She's going to come to the diner tomorrow. Sit where everyone can see her breathing."

Evelyn's hands continued their work. "Good," she said. Then, after a beat, as if swallowing once before speaking: "Your Aunt Bernice called here too. Said Joe's doubling down on stupid."

Naomi leaned on the doorframe. "He's not the only one."

Evelyn's hands stilled. "You be careful."

"I am," Naomi said. "Careful isn't quiet."

"I know," Evelyn said, surprising them both. She set the pea shell aside and rubbed her thumb over the groove it had left. "Your grandfather believed in quiet like it was religion. Your grandmother passed it down like a family recipe. I believed I was being faithful by serving it to you."

Naomi moved to the table and sat. "We ate it because we loved you."

Evelyn's eyes shone without falling. "I know." She pulled a dishrag from the sink and wrung it out twice, by habit. Then she caught herself and laid it flat. "I'm trying to learn a new recipe."

Naomi laughed softly. "I'll write it down for you. Flour, cream, and prayer."

Evelyn looked confused for a breath, then smiled in a way Naomi hadn't seen in years. "I can do prayer," she said.

They shelled peas side by side, the sound like soft applause.

When evening eased in, Naomi took the long way around the block to think with her feet. She passed the house where her grandparents had lived—the porch listing a little, the chain-link fence still holding back nothing. In her mind, she saw the table, the three knocks, and the dishrag doctrine. She saw Caleb at twelve, palms up, explaining gravity with such wild belief you'd have forgiven him anything. She saw Uncle Joe in the backyard at a barbecue once, sloshing beer as he told a story with too many heroes, none of them him. She remembered the moment Paul came through the gate, wearing his easy grin, and Joe's posture changed—relief and resentment twisted together like a rope.

"They'll forget by morning," Bernice had whispered then, to nobody particular, to everybody. "If we help them."

Naomi was fifteen and had taken her plate into the kitchen, crying quietly into the sink because it seemed all the women she loved were enrolled in the same school—teach the world to forget, and call it love.

A cicada screamed from somewhere overhead like a small machine chewing grief. Naomi stopped under the streetlamp nearest her grandparents' old cedar tree and wrote in her notebook by the light it made: *Grit is not loud. Grit is the next step. The small yes. The soft no. The hand that doesn't shake when you unlock your own door.*

She stood there until the words felt true in her mouth. Then she walked home.

Evelyn had left the porch light on, the kind of uncomplicated blessing Naomi accepted without argument. Inside, the house was a little cooler, a little kinder. Naomi washed her hands, dried them on the towel, and did not wring it out. She ate the peas with salt, stood at the sink, and watched her face in the small square of glass in the top of the door.

Her father's sentence rose like a buoy in a dark place. *You rest when you're done, not when you're scared.* She didn't feel done. She did feel scared. The mixture tasted like honesty.

In her room, she sat on the edge of the bed and let the day out slow down. The small things lined up in her mind in the same quiet way peas had lined up in the colander. She could count them; she could honor them; she could call them what they were—the work.

When the phone buzzed, she jumped. A message from Angel: tomorrow we raise holy trouble. Wear shoes. Another from Ruth, a second later: and bring your good voice. We'll need it.

Naomi smiled, set the phone down, and turned off the lamp. The house settled, as if it, too, had done enough for one day. The darkness was not empty; it held the town's steady breathing, the whisper of tomorrow's edges.

Grit in the small things, she told herself as sleep reached up for her one biscuit. One look, you don't look away from. One conversation you don't let die. One sister you walk around the block. One aunt you answer without swallowing yourself.

Outside, a truck rolled by and did not slow down. Naomi didn't sit up to watch it. She had done her portion of the day. She would get up and do the next one.

She would be steady where loudness failed.

She would move, even tired.

And the town would have to learn a new recipe, or go hungry.

CHAPTER 4

The Weight
of Boundaries

By the time Naomi reached the kitchen, the number of envelopes had multiplied. Evelyn had them lined in tidy ranks, each stamped, each addressed, each weighted by something small—a salt shaker, a coaster, a jar of buttons—as if the slightest breeze might conspire to spill her life onto the floor. The fan turned slowly above them, moving warm air from one corner to another like a secret passed between pews.

"You're up early," Evelyn said, eyes on her pen. "I made oatmeal."

"You always do," Naomi said. She sat. The chair creaked the way it had when she was twelve, like it remembered her weight. Evelyn slid the bowl across and laid the spoon as carefully as a nurse setting a thermometer under a tongue.

"You're walking again," Evelyn added, still not looking up. "People notice who walks where."

"I like the air."

"They'll twist it," Evelyn said, and her jaw worked once, a muscle she used to keep from saying more. "They'll say you're prowling. They'll say you're hunting trouble."

Naomi tasted cinnamon and salt, swallowed past the knot that wasn't oatmeal. "They can say what they like. I'm not going to live to keep their mouths busy."

Evelyn's glance cut up, quick as a sparrow. She opened her mouth, closed it, and opened it again. "You think you're stronger than this place."

"I think I finally know what I am," Naomi said. "And what I won't be again."

Evelyn reached for the dish rag by the sink, wrung it once out of habit, then stopped, aware of herself, of the old choreography. She laid it flat on the counter with effort, palms lingering there as if pinning something invisible.

The phone on the wall rang—a bright, old-fashioned sound that belonged to a house where news traveled fast and kindness traveled slow. Evelyn snatched it up. "Hello?" She turned her shoulder, voice lowering. "Bernice. Mmm. Yes. I know." A pause. "She's here." Another pause. "We can't make her do anything, Bernice. She's grown." Her eyes flicked to Naomi, then away. "I said I would talk to her, but—" She swallowed hard. "No. I'm not telling her to stay inside. This isn't a storm."

Naomi held her spoon still and stared at the back of her mother's neck, the thin cord of tension there like a taut clothesline. Evelyn's free hand found the rag again, wrung once, and stopped.

"I'll bring the dish by around five," Evelyn said at last, as if the last sentence might sew the rest of the conversation into something ordinary. "All right. Goodbye."

She hung up and breathed out through her nose. "Your aunt," she said, smoothing the front of her blouse, arranging her mouth. "She worries."

"She worries loud," Naomi said. "About Joe or about me?"

"About you," Evelyn said. "And about what you will make people say about… all of us."

Naomi set the spoon down. "I won't be told to be quiet to keep anybody's name clean."

"Quiet kept us safe," Evelyn said too sharply, flinching at her own edge. She folded her arms across herself like she could keep something from spilling. "When your uncle lost the farm money—when he—when Paul—" She broke off and pressed her lips thin. "You don't understand what that would have done to your grandfather. The shame."

"Shame for who?" Naomi asked, calm because anything hotter would burn them both. "For the ones who did wrong? Or for the women who carried it?"

Evelyn looked small for a moment—no posture, no tidy stacks, just a woman who had been taught to hold heavy things in a particular, painful way. "I thought silence saved us," she whispered.

"It saved reputations," Naomi said. "It didn't save Caleb."

They stood in that sentence until the fan's clicking felt like a metronome for grief. Evelyn set the rag down, flat again, careful.

"If I ask you to stop," she said finally, "what will you say?"

"I'll say no," Naomi answered. "I love you. And no."

Evelyn's eyes filled and did not spill. She nodded once, as if that were a language she'd promised herself to learn. "Thank you for telling me plain," she said, and her voice was almost a stranger's—softer, less rehearsed.

Naomi took her bowl to the sink, rinsed it, dried it on a rag, and did not wring it out. "If Bernice calls again about me," she said, not unkindly, "tell her to call me."

"She won't," Evelyn said, and the corner of her mouth pulled like a woman who knows a pattern and hates it. "But I hear you."

"I'll be back for lunch," Naomi said.

"If people say things—"

"They will," Naomi said. "And it won't belong to me."

Evelyn nodded, like a student repeating a lesson. Naomi kissed her temple and stepped into a day already staring.

The heat hadn't found its teeth yet. Naomi walked slowly enough to let the street tell on itself. Mr. Greer watered his petunias in a shirt he'd worn to paint three houses, the hose arcing as steady as his gossip. Two little girls chalked butterflies on the concrete; when Naomi passed, they stopped mid-wing and watched, then turned back to their drawing as if whatever they decided would change the weather.

Across from the diner, Mrs. Parker hung a dish towel on her line and peered over it with eyes that could count your sins and your vitamins. "Back again?" she called.

"Still," Naomi said.

"I always say women who walk alone are asking for something," Mrs. Parker declared.

Naomi smiled, unbothered. "I am. I'm asking for air." She held Mrs. Parker's gaze long enough to set the boundary gently in place. The older woman made a slight noncommittal sound and retreated into the safety of her kitchen.

At the diner, Loretta's hair defied physics, and the bell did its little alarm. The room went quiet for a heartbeat, then resumed the low negotiation people mistake for peace. Naomi claimed a stool. Loretta poured without being asked.

"Your aunt called here at six," Loretta said, voice sweet as syrup and twice as thick. "Wanted to know if I'd tell you to keep your head down. I told her my eggs don't scramble themselves, and neither do people."

"Thank you," Naomi said.

"You want trouble," Loretta added, "you go looking for me. You want peace, you still come here, but you sit by the window and eat a biscuit. Both are acceptable."

"Biscuit," Naomi said, grateful for a choice that didn't bruise.

Down at the end of the counter, Frank folded his paper with unnecessary noise. "Joe still owes half the county," he observed. "Man can't keep his mouth or his wallet shut."

"Then he ought to learn to open the right one," Loretta said without turning. "You hush."

The bell chimed again; Ruth entered on grace and Angel on momentum. They bracketed Naomi the way bookends keep a shelf steady.

"Report," Angel said, dropping a tote on the floor like she'd brought ammunition.

"Bernice called Mama," Naomi said. "Tried to deputize her to keep me inside."

Angel's eyebrows climbed. "Bernice can go on and deputize a wall."

Ruth squeezed Naomi's forearm. "How did your mother do?"

"She wrung the rag once," Naomi said. "Then she put it down."

Ruth smiled like a small victory had moved two inches closer. "That's a new hymn."

Angel cracked her knuckles—not a threat, a pep talk. "We're writing a whole new hymnal."

They ate at the counter, then carried their mugs to the corner table by the window, letting the light make halos of the dust. Sister May held court two booths away, whisper-praying with her companions the way a gardener picks worms from leaves. Naomi let the sound slide off her skin.

When they left, the bell's goodbye sounded like a held breath finally let go. On the sidewalk, the town narrowed and widened with each step. A truck rolled slowly past; Naomi knew the driver's hat even if she didn't see his eyes. He adjusted his mirror to catch them as they walked. Angel raised two fingers from her hip in a salute that meant you are seen, but not welcome.

They cut toward Lydia's and found Aunt Bernice on the porch next door, arms folded, mouth folded, everything folded except the part of her that never did. Her eyes scanned Ruth and Angel, then landed on Naomi as if the other two were weather.

"Afternoon," Bernice said. "You come by with that dish?"

"I'll bring it closer to five," Naomi said. "When you asked Evelyn to keep me inside, did you mean inside her house or inside my own mouth?"

Bernice's gaze held steady. "I meant inside common sense."

"I don't live there anymore," Naomi said pleasantly. "It was too small."

Ruth shifted, ready to soften the edges; Angel leaned, ready to sharpen them. Bernice's nostrils flared. "People are choosing sides," she said. "Family should be careful what side it's caught standing on."

"Family should be careful what it does when nobody's looking," Naomi said, gentler than the line deserved. "We'll be by with the dish."

Bernice's lips thinned. "You do that."

They left it there because some conversations are best finished with silence and a nod.

By midmorning, the heat had grown teeth. In Lydia's living room, a fan pushed air lazily, moving grief but not lifting it. Lydia's hair was up in something that might once have been a bun; her sweatshirt hung like someone else's.

"You look like you slept," Naomi said, hopeful.

"I did," Lydia said. "And then I didn't. And then I dreamed of Caleb knocking, and woke up hating everybody who isn't him."

Ruth sat beside her and passed a cold glass like communion. "Sip," she said. "Then tell us if you need us to tell you you're not crazy."

"I know I'm not crazy," Lydia said. "I'm tired." She glanced at Naomi. "Bernice called you?"

"She's calling everybody," Naomi said.

"She called me and told me to keep you from 'making a spectacle,'" Lydia said, fingers quoting in the air. "I told her I don't keep anything anymore. I barely keep breathing."

Angel whistled softly. "I love you a little extra today."

Lydia's mouth tipped upward. "Don't. I'll cry, and then I'll have to take a pill to stop, and then I won't remember you did it."

Naomi moved to the window and looked through the slats. Across the street, two of Paul's boys leaned on a car, making big shadows and bigger jokes. They weren't subtle; they weren't meant to be. "They're back," she said.

"I saw them at midnight," Lydia said. "Staring through me like windows."

"We'll be louder than they're looking," Angel said, and Ruth tapped her knee once, a reminder that loudness has timing.

They stayed until Lydia's shoulders unclenched. When they left, Naomi touched the doorframe and whispered something only wood needed to hear: *Hold*.

On the long walk home, Naomi's route detoured all on its own toward the churchyard. Hope Chapel stood with its white steeple, shouldering a sky that is often bruised. The sign out front begged stillness and advertised potato salad. Naomi climbed the little hill and leaned on the iron gate. The metal was hot under her palm.

She remembered a summer barbecue in her grandparents' yard, the heat wringing sweat from every collar. She was nine. Caleb was eleven and had decided gravity and truth worked the same way. Uncle Joe had told a story about a man who'd cheated him and a debt that would make them all rich once it was paid. Aunt Bernice had laughed too loud and then pinched Joe later when she thought nobody was looking. Paul had walked in wearing a smile that made even mosquitoes hesitate, and Joe had changed shape—shoulders looser, voice brighter, lies easier. Naomi's grandfather had knocked the table three times. *Enough*. Her grandmother had hung the rag, twice-wrung and once-folded. *Hush*. Naomi had felt the rag inside her own throat like a string being pulled. Later, she'd stood at the sink and watched Evelyn practice an apology to thin air, trying out different sentences for Bernice, for Joe, for herself.

"Good girls don't make messes," Evelyn had told the mirror.

Naomi had whispered to the steam, "Good girls don't make *this* mess," and the mirror had refused to answer.

Now, on the hill, Naomi traced the iron scrollwork with the tip of her finger until the heat forced her to let go. Two boys threw a football in the lot, trying to look older than they were. The ball thumped the signboard, and Sister May emerged from the side door with her lips pursed into scripture. Naomi left before she could turn a sermon into an argument.

She skirted the council building because some days you decide which giants you'll look in the eye. Through the glass, she saw Brother Harlan talking low to a woman from the grocery. He caught Naomi's eye and gave the slightest nod—permission or prayer or both.

At noon, Evelyn made tuna salad and placed it on the table with lettuce leaves arranged in a manner that seemed like an apology. She sat across from Naomi, folding her hands in her lap. The dish rag lay beside the sink, flat, a minor, unwrung miracle.

"I talked to Bernice again," Evelyn said. "Told her I wouldn't be the one to keep you quiet."

"Thank you," Naomi said, and meant it like water.

"She said Joe's got receipts in other people's pockets," Evelyn went on. "Said he thinks Paul owes him protection. A man like that doesn't understand the math."

"A man like that understands exactly the math," Naomi said. "He just doesn't think anyone will make him show his work."

They ate in the chambered peace that sometimes settles between two people learning each other again. Halfway through, Evelyn's shoulders softened.

"When your grandfather was a young man," she said, "he got in a fight behind the feed store. The other man said something about his father— your great-granddaddy—and your granddaddy hit him so hard, he split his own knuckles. He came home with blood on his shirt, and your grandmother cleaned it and told him, 'Next time, don't bleed where everybody can see.' He heard the wrong part. He decided the lesson was never to be seen. I married a man who believed it was noble to disappear. I taught my children to be saints by staying small."

Naomi put her fork down. "You taught us to survive."

"I taught you to hide," Evelyn said, honest like a fresh wound. "I don't want to do it anymore."

"Then don't," Naomi said. "Come with me to the listening session tomorrow."

Evelyn's face went wary, then brave, then something tender Naomi hadn't seen since she was a girl in bright scarves. "If I come," she said, "and if they say my name the way they say yours—"

"I'll stand next to you," Naomi said. "And if they say mine, you stand next to me."

Evelyn's mouth trembled. "All right," she whispered. "All right."

Ruth's screen door sang when Naomi knocked. The kitchen smelled like cinnamon and old books, like Mercy had put on an apron. Angel was spread across the counter as if she'd claimed the room by surface area alone.

"We're rehearsing," Angel announced. "Ruth says boundaries are muscles. I am working my deltoids."

Ruth rolled her eyes fondly. "We're practicing saying no without apologizing first."

Angel cleared her throat, put one hand on her hip, and addressed an imaginary Sister May. "No, you may not pray control into my life," she intoned. "You may pray for courage in your own. Now step aside, you're blocking my biscuits."

Ruth clapped slowly. "A touch aggressive, but the structure is solid."

Naomi laughed, and the sound came out brighter than the day deserved. "Teach me," she said.

Ruth nodded and took Naomi's hands. "Say it plain. No qualifiers. No explanations that open the door you just closed. Ready?"

Naomi inhaled. "No," she said, then frowned. "Feels like a pebble."

"Again," Ruth said.

"No."

"Again."

"No."

Angel grinned. "Again—but with your mama's cheekbones."

Naomi tilted her chin and let herself grow half an inch. "No," she said, and the syllable lengthened into something useful.

"Good," Ruth said. "Now put a boundary on it."

Naomi took a breath. "No, I won't be quiet. I won't meet with Paul in private. I won't answer questions asked from across the street. If you want to talk, you come to the meeting like the rest of us."

Angel whooped. "And bring snacks if you do."

Ruth squeezed Naomi's fingers. "That's a line. Keep it."

They role-played the evening to boost their confidence. Ruth went to wash her hands; Angel leaned close. "Want me to go tell Evelyn all that for you?" she asked, wicked and loyal.

"No," Naomi said, and smiled because she didn't need Angel to fight this one.

On the way home, the sky bruised purple in the east and threatened rain it wouldn't deliver. Naomi stopped by Mikey's Garage to ask about the noise in Evelyn's fanbelt and left with a promise and a grease thumbprint on her forearm that felt like belonging. She cut through the alley behind Murphy's; the sour tang of last night's beer clung to the bins. A voice inside rose and fell—Joe's—telling the kind of story that improved with each telling until it couldn't bear its own weight.

She thought of going in. She kept walking.

At Bernice's, Naomi climbed the porch and set the casserole dish down on a wicker chair. Before she could knock, the door opened.

"Come to make a point?" Bernice asked, lips tight, eyes sharper than she meant to let them be.

"Came to return what's yours," Naomi said, because she was practicing the art of short sentences that didn't invite company. "We're bringing Mama to the meeting tomorrow."

Bernice's arms crossed without consulting her. "People who like the sound of their own mouths love meetings."

"So do people who've never been allowed one," Naomi said. "We're going to be heard."

Bernice's gaze flicked down the street and back. "You make a mess, you clean it."

"I am," Naomi said. "I'm cleaning it where everyone can see."

She left before the surety could turn to argument.

The porch light at Evelyn's glowed like a low candle. Inside, the house had settled; the day had thinned. Naomi found her mother at the sink, rinsing a plate, the rag lying beside it like a retired soldier.

"Bernice knows we're coming," Naomi said.

Evelyn turned off the water. "Then she'll bring a hat."

They smiled, weary and true. Naomi reached for the rag and folded it once, twice, not wringing it, just making it neat. "There are some things I won't do," she said, counting them softly like beads: "I won't meet Paul alone. I won't keep secrets from men who like the sound of their own voice. I won't answer questions shouted from porches. I won't let anybody use your love to leash me."

Evelyn nodded as if each clause was a post set into fresh concrete. "And I won't ask you to be quiet," she said. "Even if it scares me."

They stood there with their new liturgy between them, not a dishrag, not three knocks, but something like a covenant.

A rap sounded at the door—three knuckles, polite as a salesperson. Naomi and Evelyn looked at each other; Naomi went, spine remembering its practice. She opened to Sister May, bright as a Sunday hat and twice as stiff.

"Evening," Sister May said. "We have a concern in the women's circle—"

"No," Naomi said, calm and clean. "Not on my porch. I'll see you at the meeting."

Sister May blinked, rearranged her mouth, and clutched her purse like scripture. "We only want unity."

"Then bring honesty," Naomi said, and eased the door shut with the kindness you use on a wind that would like to come in and gossip with your curtains.

Evelyn stood in the kitchen, hands to her chest like a woman who had heard a note she'd been searching for. "That was—" She shook her head. "That was beautiful."

"It was short," Naomi said, and felt the power of the brevity. "That's the point."

They finished the evening in the living room, feet tucked under, old lamp glowing, as if the house wanted to practice what it would be like to hold peace that didn't cost anyone their voice. Before bed, Naomi stood in front of the small mirror in her room and said no three more times, each one a little rounder in her mouth.

When she lay down, the darkness didn't press as much. Somewhere, a truck rolled past and didn't slow down. Somewhere, a man told a story, and no one believed him. Somewhere, Ruth wrote a list, and Angel set an alarm labeled 'Raise Holy Trouble.' In the hall, Evelyn paused outside Naomi's door and didn't need to say anything through the crack.

Grit isn't loud, her father used to say. It shows up. It stands. It holds.

Naomi slid one hand under her pillow and found the notebook there, the weight of a small, right thing. *Let go and set boundaries,* she wrote in the dark, feeling each word through the pen. *No is a door you get to keep. Love is the lock you turn from the inside.*

She clicked the pen closed, set it on the nightstand, and let the house breathe.

Tomorrow, I will try to push.

She would not move.

Not off her line.

CHAPTER 5

Waiting on the Storm

The storm still hadn't broken. It was morning, but the sky pressed low, pewter and swollen, clouds dragging their feet like children who didn't want to go where they were told. Naomi stood at the kitchen window, coffee warming her hands, listening to thunder roll in the distance and never quite arrive.

Evelyn had set a mixing bowl on the counter, sleeves rolled back. Flour dusted her forearms, pale against skin that had seen too many summers of Southern sun. Naomi blinked—bread. She hadn't seen her mother make bread in years. Evelyn always said she didn't have the patience for it.

"You hate baking," Naomi said.

"I hate waiting," Evelyn corrected, jabbing a wooden spoon into the bowl. "But sometimes waiting is the only work you can do."

Naomi raised an eyebrow. "What changed?"

Evelyn didn't look up. "You did."

The words sat heavy in the air. Naomi turned back to the window, tracing raindrops that weren't falling. "I don't want to wait," she said. "Not anymore."

Evelyn kneaded the dough with a rhythm that belonged to her alone. "Neither did your brother."

The name landed like it always did—sudden, sharp, alive. Naomi's throat closed. She remembered Caleb bursting through doors, blurting out questions, refusing to hush. *Truth is meant to run,* he'd said once, "*so either chase it or get out of the way.*"

"Caleb didn't rush," Naomi murmured. "He just refused to be still."

Evelyn's hands stilled on the dough. She wiped her palms on the rag, once, twice, then forced herself to lay it flat. "That refusal is why he's gone."

Naomi spun, anger flashing. "No, Mama. Silence is why he's gone."

The words cracked between them. Evelyn flinched, then straightened her shoulders. "You'll learn patience one way or another. Better by bread than by grief."

Naomi looked at the towel covering the rising dough, its slow lift invisible but sure. She wanted to yank it off, to demand it grow faster, to prove control was possible. Instead, she left the kitchen before she betrayed herself.

Lydia

The curtains in Lydia's apartment were drawn, the room dim, the air thick with lemon cleaner over stale coffee. Lydia sat wrapped in a blanket, though the day was warm; her knees were pulled up, as if she were trying to keep herself inside.

"You look better," Naomi tried.

"You always say that," Lydia muttered. "And it's always a lie."

Naomi perched on the couch's edge. "You promised you'd come to the diner today."

"I will. Tomorrow."

"Lyd, it *is* tomorrow."

Lydia's eyes flashed, sudden and sharp. "You can't rush me. You always think that if you push hard enough, the door opens. Some of us aren't doors, Naomi. We're walls."

Naomi's throat ached. "Walls crumble."

"And sometimes they hold the house up!" Lydia snapped, voice breaking. She grabbed for her coffee and nearly spilled it. The pill bottle on the table rattled, loud in the quiet.

Naomi reached out and caught her hand. Lydia tried to pull back, then sagged, trembling. Naomi held on until the shaking slowed.

"I'm not rushing you," Naomi whispered. "I just don't want silence to win."

Lydia's chin quivered. "Then sit with me in the quiet until I can stand."

They sat, the only sounds the hum of the fridge and the unsteady tick of the fan. Naomi glanced at the console table. A shoebox of photographs sat half open. She reached instinctively and pulled one free—Caleb, grinning, arm around Lydia, summer sunlight in his hair.

Lydia snatched it away as if it were on fire. "Don't," she hissed, shoving the box closed. "I can't look at them. Not now."

Naomi wanted to argue, but Lydia's eyes were wild. She stayed quiet, letting the photo remain hidden, letting the silence fill the room like a tide. Sometimes waiting was the only kindness you could give.

***

Murphy's Bar

Naomi hadn't planned to stop, but Murphy's door was open a crack and her uncle's voice rolled through, too loud, too eager. She stepped inside, the air stale with the smell of beer and sweat.

Uncle Joe leaned on the bar, one hand clutching a glass, the other waving like a preacher's. "Paul owes me," he crowed. "Owes *all of us*. That's old debt, family debt. Caleb knew it, too, God rest him. Kid just couldn't keep his mouth shut."

Naomi froze, blood rushing in her ears.

A younger man at the bar shifted uncomfortably. "Joe, maybe don't drag the dead into it."

Joe's laugh rattled. "Dead or not, truth's truth. Caleb tried to make it fast. The world doesn't like fast truth."

Naomi saw Caleb in her mind's eye—fifteen, fists clenched, telling Joe, *You can't drink the debt away. You can't laugh it gone.* Evelyn had hushed them both, scolded Naomi for repeating it.

Now Joe grinned, sloppy and proud, telling lies over his beer. Naomi turned and walked out before she put her hands on him.

Ruth & Angel

At Ruth's house, the storm pressed but still held. Ruth sat at the table, weighing sugar with her careful hands. Angel drummed a restless rhythm with her fingers.

"Patience," Ruth said. "Seeds grow roots before you see green. The work happens underground."

"Patience is what abusers depend on," Angel countered. "They count on us to wait, to pray, to hush. That's how silence wins."

Naomi rubbed her temples. "Which is it, then? Wait or push?"

"Both," Ruth said calmly. "You wait on what you cannot hurry—like Lydia finding her feet. And you push what pretends it's too heavy to move—like Paul."

Angel leaned in. "Don't confuse patience with permission. That's their trick. Make you wait until you forget you wanted more."

Naomi's chest ached. "What if I'm too tired for both?"

Ruth's eyes softened. "That's why we stand next to you. One holds patience, one holds urgency, and together we keep you upright."

Naomi's throat thickened. She had no words, only the knowledge that these two women kept her from collapsing into either extreme.

The Garden

By evening, the sky was nearly black with storm. Naomi knelt in the small patch of earth behind Evelyn's house, dirt cool and damp under her nails. She pressed seeds into the soil—peas, tomatoes, whatever Evelyn had saved—and covered them gently.

"You won't rush this," she whispered.

The first fat drop of rain splashed onto her arm, then another. The storm had finally decided.

She sat back on her heels, soaked, face lifted. Caleb's voice echoed in her memory: *If you yank too soon, you lose both worm and fish. Wait for the pull, Naomi. Wait for it to be real.*

She closed her eyes. Ruth's calm, Angel's fire, Evelyn's trembling, Lydia's fragility, Joe's lies, Bernice's warnings, Paul's smirk—all swirled in her chest.

Naomi pulled out her notebook, rain spotting the paper. She wrote in quick strokes:

Don't rush what you're meant to receive. Truth doesn't bloom faster if you shout at the dirt. But silence doesn't feed it either. I will wait. But I won't stop. Waiting is not quitting. And when the pull comes, I won't miss it.

She closed the notebook, pressed it to her chest, and let the rain soak her hair flat.

Tomorrow would come. Tomorrow would test her. Tomorrow would demand more grit than today.

But tonight, she received the storm.

CHAPTER
6

Family Ties,
Fractured

Millstone was smaller than Naomi remembered, and bigger too. Smaller because each block seemed to hold less life than it once had—houses leaning, paint peeling, front yards gone to dust. Bigger because every set of eyes added weight, stretching time with each stare, each whispered name that reached her before the lips even closed.

She walked slowly down Main Street, letting herself be carried away by the rhythm of the place. The hardware store still had the same bent awning, the grocery store was still plastered with signs for canned sales across its windows, and the post office flag still snapped against a pole that should have been replaced years ago. But it wasn't just the sameness that pressed against her—it was the way people moved. Too careful. Too watchful.

Mrs. Greer was unloading groceries into her trunk, her thin wrists trembling under the weight of a sack of potatoes. She looked up, saw Naomi, and her mouth pinched. "Back again?" she asked, though Naomi hadn't left in hours.

"Still here," Naomi answered evenly.

A man coming out of the barber shop spat in the gutter as she passed, not aiming at her, but making sure the sound landed. Two teenage girls crossed the street, giggling too loudly until Naomi realized the laughter wasn't about each other.

Millstone walked in groups even when it was alone. Every face carried the echo of a family line, the voice of a father, the shame of a mother, the debts of an uncle. Naomi carried hers too, and today she was going straight into the heart of it.

The path to Bernice's house felt longer than it should have. Naomi's body remembered childhood walks—the scrape of her shoes on the sidewalk, the smell of chicken frying drifting from kitchen windows, the sting of Caleb's elbow in her ribs when he dared her to run the last block.

She thought of Sundays in that house, long tables groaning with food, laughter pitched a little too high to hide the tension that lay under it. She thought of her grandparents at the head, her grandfather's hand poised like a gavel, her grandmother's rag ready to signal the end of any truth that threatened to show.

One Sunday in particular rose unbidden. Naomi had been eleven, small enough to sit on the edge of her chair, big enough to know her voice mattered. Joe had been drinking, loud with stories of debts and promises of money that was coming "any day now." Caleb, thirteen and restless, had dared to laugh.

"Money doesn't just fall from the sky, Uncle Joe," he'd said, grin wide, eyes dancing. "If it did, you'd have caught it by now."

The table had stilled. Bernice had gasped. Evelyn had shot Naomi a look that welded her tongue to the roof of her mouth. Grandpa's three knocks rapped like thunder, and Grandma had wrung the rag, twisting silence back into place.

Caleb hadn't stopped. "Maybe if we stopped waiting for Paul to fix everything, we'd fix it ourselves."

Joe had lurched half out of his chair. Evelyn had grabbed Caleb's arm so hard that Naomi remembered the bruise later. The rag had dripped water onto the floor. And Naomi had sat there, swallowing words, learning the taste of them lodged in her chest.

Now, as she stood at Bernice's porch decades later, she still felt that ache—the silence her family had served as faithfully as supper.

The door opened before she knocked.

"Naomi." Bernice's tone carried surprise, but not welcome. She looked put together—lipstick neat, hair set—but her eyes were tired in ways she couldn't powder away.

"I came by with the dish," Naomi said, holding out the wrapped pan.

Bernice took it, set it aside, then motioned her in. The living room smelled of lemon polish layered over the scent of tobacco. On the end table, a stack of bills sat half-hidden under a church bulletin.

Uncle Joe lounged in his chair, boot off, sock stained, glass in hand. He raised it in a sloppy salute. "Well, if it ain't Naomi LeBlanc, the town prophet."

"Joe," Bernice warned.

"What?" He grinned, wide and yellow. "She came to preach. Might as well let her get it over with."

Naomi didn't move further inside. She stood near the doorway, her hands steady. "I didn't come to preach. I came to tell you I won't be quiet anymore."

Joe's laugh rattled. "Quiet keeps families safe. Quiet keeps us fed. You think Paul's been running this town on prayers? He feeds us, and you don't bite the hand that feeds you."

Naomi's chest burned. "You call it feeding. I call it choking."

The words sliced through the air. Bernice's lips pressed tight. "Don't start, Naomi. Not in front of the children."

Two figures hovered in the hall—Micah and Tess. Micah shifted his weight, tall but hesitant, shoulders hunched as though expecting a blow. Tess stood rigid, arms crossed, chin high, eyes sharp with judgment.

"They're old enough to hear," Naomi said softly.

Joe slammed his glass down on the table, liquid sloshing. "Hear what? More speeches? Caleb tried that. And look where he is now."

Naomi's breath caught. "Don't you dare use his name like that."

"Why not?" Joe sneered. "He opened his mouth, and the dirt shut it for him. You want the same?"

The room pulsed with silence. Bernice stood, stepped between them, and smoothed her skirt with shaking hands. "Naomi, you can't drag us all into this. We've worked too hard to keep our heads above water."

"You've worked too hard to pretend the water isn't rising," Naomi shot back.

Micah's hands clenched at his sides. Tess hissed, "You think you're better than us."

Naomi turned her gaze on them both. "No. I think you can be better. That's the difference."

Bernice wrung the dish rag once, hard. The sound echoed like a gunshot. Tess flinched; Micah's jaw tightened.

Naomi's throat ached, but her voice was steady. "I love you. But I won't be quiet for you. Not anymore."

Bernice's face twisted—fear, pain, pride all tangled. "Then may God protect you. Because I can't."

Naomi turned for the door. Behind her, she heard Tess mutter, "She'll ruin us." Micah whispered, barely audible, "Maybe she'll save us."

The storm outside had not broken, but the air was heavy with waiting.

Ruth's kitchen was warm with the scent of cinnamon and a sense of steadiness. Naomi sank into a chair, shoulders heavy. Ruth slid a cup of tea toward her; Angel leaned on the counter, arms crossed, fire in her eyes.

"So?" Angel demanded. "How bad?"

"They still think silence is loyalty," Naomi said.

"And you told them no," Ruth said, a statement more than a question.

"I told them no," Naomi echoed.

Angel slammed her hand on the counter. "Good. One by one, Naomi. First the family, then the town, then Paul. Let them choke on their silence while we breathe."

Naomi sipped the tea, warmth filling her chest. "It doesn't feel like breathing. It feels like breaking."

Ruth reached across and laid her hand over Naomi's. "Breaking is what makes room for new growth."

Angel's grin flashed. "And breaking is loud. Don't forget that part."

Naomi thought of Caleb, of Evelyn, of Bernice's rag twisted in her fists, of Joe's bitter laugh, of Micah's whispered words. The ties of family were still there, frayed, bleeding, ready to snap.

And maybe that was the only way something new could be tied.

CHAPTER 7

The Diner Divides

Loretta set the mug down harder than necessary. It rattled on the saucer and steadied.

"You hungry for eggs or arguments?" she asked.

"Eggs," Naomi said. "Arguments seem to be on special."

A couple in the corner smirked. Sister May sat two booths over with Mrs. Talley and Nadine Crowley, their purses bunched up like chaperones. May's voice carried as if aided by a tiny microphone only self-righteousness could hear.

"Unity," she announced, "is what God prescribes in times of turmoil. Loose tongues are a plague. Women who stir are often... lonely."

Nadine made a sympathetic mouth. "Mmm."

Mrs. Talley tried out a new sound—"tsk"—and seemed to like the way it felt.

At the counter, Frank Bentlee folded his paper loudly. "Paul kept this town afloat through two recessions," he told the room. "Girl comes back and thinks she knows better than a man who built half our roofs."

A younger man two stools down said, without looking up, "Those roofs leak."

"Shut your mouth, Tyler," Frank growled.

Loretta slid a plate in front of Naomi—biscuits with gravy that had the color of a good decision. "Eat," she said to Naomi. Then, louder: "And if you got something to say, say it where your mouth can be seen."

Tyler flushed. "Just saying folks act like Paul's a miracle when he's just a man with a hand out both directions."

Sister May pivoted in the booth. "Young men would do better to respect their elders."

"And elders would do better to stop hiding behind Bible words," Loretta shot back, sweet as pie with a razor under it. "Naomi, you want jam?"

"Please," Naomi said, even as her heart climbed a rung in her throat. She could feel the room leaning toward a cliff.

The bell chimed. Uncle Joe swaggered in like a man who'd won a prize he hadn't bought. He scanned, found Naomi, and smiled with a wide grin. "Well now," he said. "If it ain't the reason folks can't finish breakfast."

"Joe," Loretta warned.

"What?" He swung onto a stool two seats from Naomi. "I'm here for eggs and entertainment." He turned to Frank. "Tell 'em how Paul covered that roof at the high school when the county ran out of money."

Frank beamed as if he'd hammered it himself. "Man knows how to get things done."

"Man knows how to send a bill later," Tyler muttered.

Sister May raised her voice. "We are not here to slander God's provision."

Naomi set her fork down. "God's provision doesn't come with hush money," she said. It came out calm. It didn't wobble. "If help means I'm not allowed to tell the truth, it isn't help. It's a leash."

Joe slapped the counter. "Listen to her. She thinks she's Joan of Arc."

"Joan of Ark kept her mouth shut," Frank said, which is not what she did, and two people at the back snorted.

Loretta tapped a spoon against the coffee pot, a bright ping that made everybody blink. "House rules," she said. "If you're going to use the Lord to win an argument, you'd better sound at least ten percent like

Him. No gossip. No threats. And if you say Paul's name, you say Naomi's, too, because we're not pretending she isn't here."

The room recalibrated—some faces softer, some sharpening.

A boy in a busboy apron came out from the kitchen with a tub of dishes. He couldn't have been more than sixteen. He looked at Naomi like she'd stepped off a page in a book they hadn't assigned yet.

"My mama says you're trouble," he blurted.

Loretta hissed, "Evan."

He went red. "I didn't mean— I just mean she says you'll make it worse before it gets better."

Naomi met his eyes. "She's probably right."

A few people laughed—the nervous kind, but laughter all the same. Sister May bristled; Joe rolled his eyes.

Naomi stood. The scrape of the stool on tile was scandalously loud. "If you need me quiet to be comfortable, I can't help you," she said, looking at no one and everyone. "If you need me to be honest to be free, I will sit with you until the coffee goes cold."

Loretta reached across the counter and squeezed Naomi's hand. "Breakfast is on me," she said. "And so is backup."

Outside, heat smacked her face and blessed her at the same time. The bell jingled as the door swung shut behind her. Voices rose again. This time, they didn't sound like secrets. They sounded like a town arguing with itself out loud for the first time in a long time.

Naomi stood on the sidewalk and let the sun lay a hand on her shoulder.

The church would be next.

CHAPTER
8

*The Church
Sermon*

Sunday carried heat like a heavy hymn. Naomi and Evelyn walked the block to Hope Chapel together, their steps almost—but not quite—in rhythm. Evelyn had insisted they arrive early, "so we don't look like we're sneaking in."

The chapel's white clapboard shone too bright for August; up close, the paint could not hide the wood's old lines. The marquee read: **BE STILL AND KNOW** on one line, **LISTENING SESSION TUESDAY – POTLUCK TO FOLLOW** below it. Listening and potato salad. Millstone loved to plate them together.

Inside, the sanctuary swelled with the smell of pressed cotton and hymnals. Fans flicked, bones creaked, whispers threaded the pews in tidy stitches. Naomi slid into the third row with Evelyn, the wood beneath her thighs polished by generations of fidgeting. The air carried her name the way a current carries a leaf—at first gently, then with purpose.

Reverend Carter stepped into the pulpit with a caution that looked like reverence until you watched it too long. He laid his hand on the Bible and breathed through his nose.

"We are living in a season of unrest," he said, voice smooth as a sealed envelope. "The enemy prowls, seeking whom he may devour. And often he begins with the tongue."

A murmur rolled. Sister May tilted her hat like a judge's gavel. Naomi kept her eyes forward and her jaw loose. The enemy doesn't need to prowl, she thought. He's been invited to supper every Sunday and given seconds.

Carter read from James: *The tongue is a small spark that sets a forest ablaze.* He paused on *spark* as if the pause itself were a sermon. "Some of us would do well to remember that."

Evelyn stiffened. Naomi's fingers twitched toward her mother's hand and then flattened against her skirt.

A memory rose, loud with the bright certainty of youth: Caleb at fourteen, slipping Naomi a folded scrap during a sermon—*God doesn't fear sparks. He made fire.* Evelyn had caught it, drained the ink with one look, and hissed, "Don't you shame us in church." Caleb had whispered—careful, but not cautious enough—"Maybe church ought to be ashamed of itself." Afterward, Grandpa's knuckles had rapped the kitchen table three times. Grandma's rag had twisted in her fist until water slicked the floor.

"Unity is precious," Carter continued. "We must guard it. Resist those who tear it—" a glance like a thread drawn quick through fabric, "—even with good intentions."

Even with good intentions. The hedge clipped around the truth.

Naomi studied the wood grain of the pew in front of her, knowing that faces would betray her. Somewhere behind, Mrs. Talley hummed agreement. Farther back, a child whispered, "Who's Naomi?" and a mother replied, "Hush," with the kind of hush that was a family heirloom.

The hymns were safe ones. The choir sang without looking left. As the benediction fell, the sanctuary fractured into small rivers of talk that flowed toward the doors and pooled in the vestibule.

"Morning, Sister," Deacon Whitlow said, materializing with a smile that had the moral temperature of tepid tea. "We're praying for a quiet spirit in you."

"Prayer is good," Naomi said. "Quiet isn't a fruit of the Spirit."

Whitlow blinked, recalculated, and nodded.

"Naomi," Sister May sang, arriving with two women who carried purses like shields. "We love peacemakers. Peacemakers are blessed."

"They are," Naomi agreed. "And they're loud. They say the hard thing first."

A shape filled the side of her vision. Paul. Not grand, not gaudy—never that. Crisp shirt, tidy smile, a man who looked like a solution from far away. Reverend Carter shook his hand at the bottom of the steps with the care you give a delicate instrument. Paul's eyes slid over Naomi the way men look at fences and calculate where to cut.

"Let's be mindful," Carter added to no one and everyone, "of how we represent this body."

"We are," Naomi said, but the sentence was for Evelyn. "We will be."

On the lawn, Bernice tightened her hand around Tess's arm. Tess stared with a heat Naomi recognized from mirrors. Micah stood a pace off, hands in pockets, jaw set—not defiant, exactly, but finally choosing to stand somewhere.

Joe held court near the hedge, voice pitched for catchers, not listeners. "Folks who love sparks burn their own houses down," he declared, and three men nodded like they'd read it in Proverbs.

Evelyn's breath shortened. "They're saying your name like it's a warning," she whispered. "Like it's something you catch."

Naomi guided her down the steps. Sun and heat met them like something honest. "You don't have to hear them today," she said. "I'll hear them, and I'll hand you only what won't poison."

They moved past Paul. He inclined his head, cordial as a condolence. "Miss Naomi," he said. "Good to see you among us."

"I live among you," Naomi said, without stopping.

Something like amusement tilted his mouth. "For now."

Evelyn stumbled. Naomi tightened her grip and didn't look back. On the lawn behind them, the marquee letters rattled as the wind lifted. **LISTENING SESSION TUESDAY** clacked softly, as if repeating itself to the air.

Naomi did not turn. If she had, she might have seen Micah peel away from Bernice, his shoulders square like a man deciding to be taller than his fear. If she had, she might have seen Sister May's hat dip in prayer or calculation—hard to tell the difference from a distance.

Evelyn's hand trembled against Naomi's arm. Naomi steadied her mother and walked her home through a town that had stopped pretending it wasn't choosing.

The sermon was over. The message had only just begun.

CHAPTER 9

Evelyn Breaks

The Cracking Point

The house held its breath, as if it had learned not to be a witness. Evelyn sat at the kitchen table with both hands flat on the wood as if she needed to keep it from floating off. The dish towel lay folded by the sink. She stared at it the way some people stare at altars—afraid to touch, afraid not to.

"Say what you need to say," Naomi told her, taking the chair opposite, planting her feet, laying her palms down too. Two women, one table, an old covenant between them being renegotiated without a lawyer.

"When Caleb died," Evelyn began, the name scraping her throat on the way out, "I told myself it was because he would not hush. I made that lie my pillow so I could sleep. If it is true—" she swallowed, hard, "—then I am a mother who asked her son to earn his safety by being less alive."

Silence took a chair. Naomi let it. The fridge motor hummed. Somewhere outside, a truck rattled past with a muffler that had opinions.

"I told him hush the night before," Evelyn whispered. "Joe was drunk, Bernice had vinegar where her voice should be, Paul was smiling that smile men wear when they have decided something for you. Your grandfather's hand was already on the table to knock. I thought if I kept my boy small, the storm would pass." She laughed once, a thin sound. "It did not."

Naomi reached out and covered her mother's hands. Evelyn didn't pull away. Her skin was cool, then warming under Naomi's palms, heat shared like a message.

"I hear his voice when you open yours," Evelyn said. "And I am afraid they will make you pay the same price."

"I am afraid, too," Naomi answered, because choosing bravery had never meant throwing out honesty. "But fear doesn't get the keys. Not anymore."

A thump sounded against the front porch. Both women stiffened. Naomi stood, but Evelyn was faster—she crossed the room and pulled the screen open. A plain envelope lay against the threshold, unsealed and unstamped. Evelyn bent down, picked it up like it might bite, and handed it to Naomi.

Inside: a single scrap of paper. *ENOUGH.* Block letters. Ink pressed hard enough to leave grooves.

Naomi's pulse kicked, but her voice stayed level. "A love note from the cowards."

Evelyn reached for the towel and then stopped, caught herself. Her hand hovered, then lowered empty. "We'll choose what enough means," she said, as if convincing herself.

Intrusion

The rap on the screen door this time was knuckles, casual as a neighbor, wrong as a stranger. Naomi opened the door to find Joe on the porch, bookended by two men who drank their meanness quietly.

"Afternoon," Joe said, chewing his words like gum. "Heard you were collecting notes."

"We're returning them," Naomi said. "You can take this one back." She slid the scrap toward him across the porch rail.

Joe didn't look at it. "You'll ruin her," he said, eyes flicking to Evelyn, then back like a dare. "You'll drag all of us where Caleb put us—under a story nobody wants to tell."

"Caleb didn't put you anywhere," Naomi said. "He tried to get you out."

One of the men smiled without teeth. "You like meetings," he said. "I hear you got one Tuesday."

"Community listening session," Naomi said. "You should try it. Might be the first time you let your ears work."

Joe's jaw hardened. "Paul's been good to this family."

"Paul's been good to Paul," Naomi said. "And men who owe him their mouths."

Evelyn stepped forward. "Joseph," she said, and the name was a scold and a mercy. "You will not step on this porch and threaten my child. Not with your voice, and not with your silence."

Joe blinked like he hadn't expected her to speak. The men behind him shifted, the way dogs shift when they realize the fence is electric.

"You want a war?" Joe asked softly.

"No," Naomi said. "I want the truth. If that feels like war to you, that's not my fault."

Joe looked at the note on the rail as if remembering he had hands. He snatched it, crushed it, and shoved it in his pocket. "Careful," he said. "Careful is all I'm saying."

"Careful, got us here," Naomi said, and closed the screen.

The three shadows moved off the porch. Tires grated. Somewhere, a crow laughed like it had heard this all before.

The Circle Tightens

Ruth arrived ten minutes later with a tote bag and a gaze that could anchor a ship. Angel followed, wearing a look that had a sharpened edge and a soft center.

"Company?" Angel asked, eyes already sweeping the room for stories. Naomi handed her the crumpled note. Angel smoothed it, snorted, and tore it neatly in half, then quarters, then eighths. "Confetti," she declared, letting it snow into the trash. "Cheap parties get cheap decorations."

Ruth set her tote down, pulled out a spiral notebook, three highlighters, and a tin of oatmeal cookies that smelled like restraint. "We're rehearsing," she announced. "Not for them. For you. For Tuesday."

Evelyn straightened, wiped under her eyes with the heel of her hand like she could erase grief the way you erase chalk. "I'll be there," she said. "Blue dress. Front row."

Angel pointed at her as if commissioning a soldier. "And if Sister May tries to pray the volume down out of Naomi's mouth—"

"I'll say amen," Evelyn said, voice thin but steady, "and then I'll say Naomi."

Ruth smiled the small, delighted smile of a woman seeing a promise keep itself. "All right," she said. "Naomi, what will you say first?"

Naomi swallowed. The words rose and arranged themselves like they'd been practicing while she slept. "I will say my name. I will say my brother's name. I will say Paul's. I will say the ways money buys silence. I will say the ways women are asked to fold themselves in half and then in half again until they disappear. I will say that I am here to be whole."

Angel's grin showed teeth. "Write it," she said. "Write it now."

Naomi wrote. The pen bled truth into paper like the paper had been thirsty.

They practiced. Ruth timed Naomi with a kitchen clock that ticked commandingly. Angel interrupted with heckles so real that Naomi's skin prickled. Evelyn interrupted with looks she had invented when

Naomi was seven and testing boundaries; now they meant "go," not "stop."

Between runs, Naomi wandered to the window and pushed the curtain with two fingers. The street watched back, as always, but something had shifted. A boy on a bike slowed and didn't hide it. Mrs. Parker stood with a watering can and did not pretend to water. Across the way, Micah paused on the sidewalk like a man who had walked to a door and not yet decided whether to knock.

Naomi lifted her chin a fraction. Micah's chin answered, infinitesimal. A pact measured in millimeters.

The Escalation

The rock that hit the porch didn't break anything. That almost made it worse. It thumped against the rail and settled, wrapped in newspaper. Angel was out the door before anyone else moved, stepping onto the porch like a boxer stepping into a ring. She crouched, unwrapped. Inside lay a scrap of ledger paper older than Naomi—columns of numbers, initials, a familiar looping P at the bottom of one line like a flourish.

Ruth peered. "A debt," she said. "Or a promise."

Evelyn's breath hitched. "Your grandfather's hand," she murmured, pointing to the top margin where three faint indents sat, like someone had knocked on a table and the wood had remembered.

Naomi took the slip. *J.B.* by one entry. *C.W.* by another. *P.* at the end. Joe. Caleb. Paul? Or someone else with a P, but the shape of that letter felt smug even in pencil.

Angel scanned the street. A sedan idled two houses down, windows dark. After a beat, it rolled off with disinterest so practiced it might have been contempt.

"Proof lands on our porch," Angel said. "God has a sense of timing."

Ruth's eyebrow lifted. "Or the cowards do."

Naomi slid the slip into Ruth's notebook. "We bring it Tuesday," she said, and felt the room agree.

The knock that came next was not a rock, not a note, not a threat pretending to be a favor. It was gentle, knuckles careful. Naomi opened the door to find Micah on the step, cap in his hands like he'd borrowed it from an older life.

"Aunt Bernice sent me to say we won't come on Tuesday," he said, the words tripping. "But that's not why I came."

Evelyn moved behind Naomi. Angel leaned on the doorframe like a curtain of muscle. Ruth stayed in the kitchen and was somehow the center of the house.

Micah swallowed. "If I don't stand there, it ain't because I don't hear you," he said. "It's 'cause I live in that house and... I can't yet. But I want to. I wanted you to know I want to."

Naomi felt something in her chest loosen and hurt at the same time. "Thank you," she said, and meant it like water. "Sometimes wanting is the bravest thing a person can say out loud."

Micah nodded, relief quick across his face like a breeze. "Be careful," he muttered. "Careful don't mean quiet. Just—watch your back."

"Angel watches my back," Naomi said.

"I watch everybody's backs," Angel corrected.

Micah almost smiled. He stepped off the porch, looked both ways like a man who had learned where danger parked, and disappeared down the sidewalk that had raised him.

Evelyn shut the door and leaned her forehead against the wood. "I can hear your grandfather telling me to be sensible," she said. "I can hear my mother's rag. But louder—" she lifted her head, eyes fierce through the salt—"louder I hear Caleb."

"What's he saying?" Ruth asked.

Evelyn's mouth trembled into a line that was not a smile and not grief, something between. "He's saying: *Don't let them bury a second child while they compliment the flowers.*"

What a Vow Sounds Like

Evening leaned into the house with long shadows and a cicada chorus. Ruth left with the ledger scrap tucked in her tote like contraband. Angel left and circled back once, just to make the street memorize her face. Naomi and Evelyn sat a while in the kitchen with the lamp on, sharing the kind of quiet that is not hush, the kind that is rest.

"Blue dress?" Naomi asked finally.

Evelyn nodded. "Blue dress."

They went to her bedroom and opened the closet that had held better years and worse. Evelyn slid the hanger free. The dress was simple, the kind of blue that doesn't apologize for being itself. Evelyn held it up to her body and studied her reflection in the mirror. The woman looking back was older than grief, older than fear, older than Millstone's rules. She looked like a woman who could sit in the front row.

Back in the kitchen, Naomi opened her notebook. The page smelled faintly of rain from the last storm that hadn't fallen. She wrote:

Act I is how we learned to breathe. Tomorrow, we speak. I will say my name first so no one can define me by theirs. I will say Caleb's breath belongs to him again. I will say Paul's without flinching. I will say that silence is a vow I never took, and if someone signed my name on it, I am rescinding my consent. We will not be neat. We will be true.

She set the pen down. The house exhaled. Outside, a car passed without slowing. Somewhere, a screen door banged the way screen doors do when they believe in wind.

Evelyn laid the dish towel on the counter and smoothed it with both hands. She folded it once, then again. She did not wring. She slipped it into a drawer and closed the drawer like a ceremony.

Thunder rumbled in the distance—not the loud, holy kind yet, but the first roll that tells the sky its lines. Naomi stood and turned off the kitchen light. In the dim, their shapes held.

"Tomorrow," Evelyn said.

"Tomorrow," Naomi said back.

In the window, the marquee letters at Hope Chapel caught a stray breeze and tapped against themselves—LIS… TEN… ING—like a word remembering its purpose.

Naomi walked to her room and placed the notebook on the chair where she'd see it when she woke. She sat on the bed and let herself be tired for exactly one minute. Then she stood again, because the body remembers practice and because storms do not wait for people to feel ready.

On the porch, air gathered. Down the block, a figure paused under a streetlamp and chose to keep walking. The town had decided to be awake.

Act I had broken open. Act II stood on the front steps, hat in hand, pretending to be polite.

ACT II

The Silence Splinters

CHAPTER 10

Whispers Behind Doors

Morning came thin and gray, a curtain the sun tugged at but didn't lift. Millstone sounded like itself again—lawn mowers, a dog telling a squirrel to repent, the clink of a spoon against a jelly jar—yet everything felt a click to the left, as if the whole town had been nudged during the night and set down slightly off its marks.

Behind doors, voices practiced their shapes.

At Sister May's house, a phone sat on a coaster like a holy relic. "We're praying for the girl," she said into it, sweet as iced tea. Then, hand over the receiver: "But we will not let her set fire to this church." The women at the other end mmm-hmm'd in a rhythm that could pass for devotion if you didn't listen too close.

At the Greers', Mr. Greer folded the paper and grunted, "Paul's kept folks working." Mrs. Greer rinsed a plate that was already clean. "And the price?" she asked, so softly the plate almost swallowed the words.

On a back street two blocks off Main, a boy in a busboy apron drank cereal milk from the bowl and told his mother, "She said truth ain't a leash." His mother arched an eyebrow and said, "Truth's a mirror, baby. Folks mad at it are usually mad at themselves."

The diner, for once, woke without Loretta. In her kitchen, hair tied up in a scarf, she leveled a cake with a bread knife and muttered, "Let somebody call her a plague to my face again." She dotted the frosting, set the timer, and stared at the clock as if it owed her rent.

Near the council building, a janitor propped open a back window for air and swept the hall where the listening session would take place. He paused by the microphone stand, the cord coiled neatly on the floor like a sleeping snake. "Behave," he told it, and kept sweeping.

At Evelyn's table, the coffee was darker than usual, and the eggs were dry, which told the truth about her hands without making a fuss of it. Naomi LeBlanc buttered toast and let butter drip where it wanted, not apologizing to the plate.

"Sleep?" Naomi asked.

"Some." Evelyn's mouth shaped the word like a coin she wasn't sure she wanted to spend.

The phone rang, the sound of a dare. Evelyn did not flinch. She stood, wiped her hands, and answered. "Hello? ... Yes, Bernice. ... We will be there. ... Because I am her mother and I have decided to be." She set the receiver down like it might explode and sat up again, spine tall.

"She says I'm embarrassing the family," Evelyn said, voice steady.

"You're changing the family," Naomi said. "Embarrassment is just the sound pride makes when it loosens."

Evelyn huffed something that wasn't a laugh, but she loved it. "You always had a way of saying it."

"You just taught me the cost of saying it out loud."

They ate. Naomi watched the sunlight thread itself through the curtains and make patterns on the table—grids and lattices, like maps of choices. After a while, she took out her notebook.

"What are you writing?" Evelyn asked.

"Names," Naomi said. "And sentences that don't wobble."

"Read me one."

Naomi did. "*Silence is a vow I never took.*"

Evelyn nodded once, a blessing.

The phone rang again. Evelyn let it. It rang long enough to tell its own story, and then it stopped ringing..

"Lydia?" Naomi asked.

"Maybe," Evelyn said. "Maybe Sister May. Maybe the devil. Whoever it is can leave a message."

Lydia's blinds were drawn against the day, but not all the way. A blade of light cut across the rug and landed on a pile of laundry that had been folded, if we are generous, sometime last week. Lydia opened the door in a T-shirt that said I'M FINE in letters so big they could do the lying for her.

"You look better," Naomi said.

"You always say that," Lydia answered, and this time the edge on the words was smaller, sanded by exhaustion into something almost kind. She stepped back. "I made coffee. It tastes like a consequence."

They sat. Lydia curled one leg under her and traced the ring a mug had left on the table as if drawing could erase it.

"They're calling me," she said. "Ladies from church. Women from the school. People who never knew my number are suddenly knowing it. Telling me to 'think about unity' and 'pray for peace' and 'please don't go Tuesday because it will only make it worse.'"

"What did you say?"

"I said I don't know yet. Because it's true." She looked up, naked in the honesty of it. "I don't know if I can stand in a room where Joe's mouth is and Paul's men are, and the whole town's eyes make me smaller. But I want to be the kind of person who can."

Naomi swallowed. "Wanting counts."

Lydia laughed, briefly, surprised. "It does not."

"It does," Naomi said. "It's the door before the door."

Lydia grew quiet. "I keep thinking about Caleb," she said. "How loud he was. How loud you are." She frowned at her hands. "I keep thinking about all the noises I made to cover the sound of my own heart."

Naomi reached across the table and pressed two fingers to Lydia's wrist. "It's still there," she said. "Loud enough."

They made a deal, as formal as any contract spoken between friends who had almost broken and decided not to: Lydia would not promise to come on Tuesday, but if she stayed home, she would pray out loud, so God would hear her voice and remember it belonged to her.

When Naomi left, the blinds were still mostly closed, but that blade of light had shifted and landed on the couch as if it meant to sit awhile.

On Oak Street, laughter leaked from Bernice's house—the high, brittle kind that meant nothing funny had happened. Naomi didn't plan to stop. Then she heard Joe's name in a tone that did not bother to be careful, and her feet made a decision without asking permission.

At the porch, she froze. The front windows were cracked for air; the voices came out thin as a rumor.

"I said we are not going," Bernice snapped.

"We?" Tess shot back. "You mean *you*. You mean you won't go and you don't want us to have a mouth you can't manage."

"Watch it," Joe warned, and the warning slurred without alcohol, which was new and therefore worse. "You don't bite the hand."

"I'm not biting," Tess said. "I'm naming." Her breath hitched on the last word, telling Naomi that someone had taught her to be brave yesterday.

Micah's voice came next, low. "I'll stand in the back. Nobody has to see me."

"They'll see you," Bernice said, exhausted. "They'll see you and they'll see me. We are a we in this house."

Silence, then the soft thud of something set down. Naomi pictured the dishrag. She pictured Bernice's hands.

"Naomi is going to ruin us," Bernice said finally, but there was no heat left in it, only a plea aimed at a God who hadn't chosen sides.

Micah again, the sound of a boy deciding to be a man and hating that it cost him something. "Maybe she'll save us."

Naomi retreated before her shadow told on her. On the sidewalk, she breathed shallowly and then deeply, counting to eight like Ruth had taught her when the world came hot and fast and asked her mouth to run ahead of her mind. She kept walking.

At the corner, two girls on bikes swerved close enough to make a point and then laughed themselves brave. Naomi lifted a hand in peace. They did not return it, but they also did not ride away as quickly as they had intended. Progress looks like that sometimes—a slower escape.

At Ruth's, the screen door creaked a welcome it reserved for certain people. Angel sat at the table with a legal pad and the posture of a woman who collects debts for God. Ruth laid out three mugs and a plate of cookies, because grace travels better when it's sugared.

"Roll call," Angel said. "We got two elders who'll speak. One of them's Ms. Oates—remember, her son got laid off after refusing a 'favor?' She's ready to name it. We have a nurse who will discuss the clinic's process for choosing who receives samples. We got a janitor with a spine like an oak—he'll whisper in my ear and I'll shout, we know the arrangement."

Ruth opened a little notebook and made check marks like a conductor tapping a baton. "We will sit together," she said. "People are creating their own choir—let ours harmonize with courage."

Naomi told them about Lydia. About Bernice's window. About the blade of light on a couch.

Ruth listened with her eyes and her hands, nodding, smoothing, patting the table once when she especially approved. "God loves a town that argues toward the truth," she said. "He loves it more than a town that sings itself to sleep."

Angel drew a square on her pad and divided it into four equal parts. "Teams," she said. "We walk together, we leave together. If anybody gets mouthy near the door, they have to get mouthy at me." She smiled, feral and fond. "Nobody likes that job."

Naomi laughed. It felt like stretching a muscle she'd almost forgotten she owned.

Ruth slid a folded paper across the table. "A letter came to my porch," she said, apologetic like she'd tracked in mud. "No return address. I think you should see it."

Naomi unfolded the single sheet. REMEMBER WHO OWNS YOU, the letters said, big as a billboard, ugly as a habit.

Angel took it, tore it clean in half, then into quarters, and finally into eighths. "New confetti," she announced, letting the bits fall into the trash. "We only keep invitations worth attending."

Ruth arched an eyebrow. "We are attending to our souls," she said. "The rest can wait."

The three of them prayed. Not the kind of prayer you say when you want to sound like you belong in a pew. The kind you say when you are a person with lungs and you need air.

When they rose, they were not taller, but they were steadier in ways that matter more.

The afternoon learned how to be evening and kept it to itself. Naomi walked home with the kind of tired that respects itself. On the porch, Evelyn sat with her hands in her lap, not twisting, not performing. The phone rang again. Evelyn reached, picked it up, and pressed the speaker button so the house could hear the truth with her.

"Evelyn," Reverend Carter said, his voice treated for kindness, "I wanted to offer a word of caution. To protect your family. To protect Naomi. I worry the meeting will… inflame."

"Inflame what?" Evelyn asked, calm as a clock.

"Old wounds. Old… resentments."

"Wounds fester when you don't open them," Evelyn said. "I'm going." She let the silence ride a moment. "And so is my daughter."

Carter cleared his throat. "You know I care for your household."

"I know you care for comfort," Evelyn said, and to her credit, it came out as diagnosis, not an insult. "Good night, Reverend."

She pressed the button. The line went dead without drama.

Naomi wanted to clap. She did not. She sat beside her mother and let the porch understand new rules.

Down the street, Micah walked past without looking up. He did not stop, but his hands were out of his pockets, palms open to the air like a man practicing honesty with the weather.

"Tomorrow," Evelyn said.

"Tomorrow," Naomi said.

Dusk laid a lavender hand over the council building. Naomi cut through the lot like a local and found the back window propped open again, the janitor's broom leaned against the wall like a tired soldier. Inside, men moved chairs into rows that spelled out "order" with their legs. Naomi stood in the grass and listened through the slit of air the window allowed.

"...limit comments to two minutes," a voice said. Not Paul. A man who liked rules because they made him feel taller.

"And if she tries a speech?" another voice asked.

"We are all for speeches," a third said, amused. "We just choose which ones count."

Then the voice she knew like a splinter: Paul. Warm, practiced. "We'll keep it calm," he said. "We'll thank people for their passion. We'll remind them of our long history of unity. And we'll close early if we must."

"If she names you?" the rule-lover asked.

Paul laughed, a sound you could pour on pancakes. "Then I'll pray."

Chairs scraped. Someone tested the microphone: one two, one two. It coughed to life and went quiet again.

Naomi's heart beat once hard against her sternum and then behaved. She turned from the window, wrote in her notebook, tore the page, folded it, slid it into her pocket like a secret she planned to make public.

On her way home, she passed Hope Chapel. The marquee shivered in a breeze that hadn't introduced itself to the rest of the street. **LISTENING SESSION TUESDAY**, it said, then said it again softly as the letters clacked together—LISTENING LISTENING LISTENING—as if practice could make it true.

She reached the porch. Evelyn had left the lamp on. Inside, the dish towel slept in its drawer. Naomi washed her hands like a ritual, the day rinsing off in ribbons, and then sat on the edge of her bed with the notebook open and the pen warm in her fingers.

Behind doors, they whisper, she wrote. *Tomorrow we will say it where the roof hears. If unity needs my silence to survive, it will have to die and be reborn as something honest. I will say my name first. I will say Caleb's next. I will say Paul's without trembling. And when they time me, I will give them two minutes that weigh a lifetime.*

She closed the book. The house breathed. Far off, thunder remembered its lines. In the small square of night outside her window, a single moth battered itself against the lamplight, insisting on brightness even when it hurt.

Naomi lay back and let the ceiling be her sky. Millstone settled around her, not asleep exactly, but practicing. Behind doors, mouths made shapes. Tomorrow, they'd learn how those shapes sounded in the open air.

CHAPTER 11

A Family
of Ghosts

The house was too quiet. Not the peace-and-tea kind, but the kind that settles like dust and waits to be inhaled. Naomi LeBlanc sat at the kitchen table long after Evelyn had gone to bed, staring at the drawer where the rag used to live. She didn't open it. Let the relic sleep. Ghosts don't need props to speak.

When sleep finally took her, it came with knocks—one, two, three—echoing down a hallway that didn't have walls. She woke with the taste of old water in her mouth.

Morning found Evelyn in the doorway with coffee and a face that hadn't finished deciding how brave it felt. "I dreamed of my father," she said. "He could look at you and sew your lips together without lifting a needle."

"What did he say?" Naomi asked.

"Nothing," Evelyn answered, surprised at her own answer. "He just knocked. Three times. And I remembered being a girl who tried to beat him to the table so he wouldn't have to." She swallowed. "I carried that knock into every room. I taught you to listen for it even when it wasn't there."

"We can stop carrying," Naomi said.

Evelyn stared at the mug. "Ghosts don't like being denied."

"They don't like being named, either," Naomi said. "We can do both."

Evelyn's mouth twitched. "You always had a way of saying the hard thing like it was a recipe."

Caleb's room smelled like a drawer left closed too long. Naomi opened the window and let August force itself in. Dust motes rose and made a galaxy out of what they had left behind: baseball cap on the bedpost, one shoelace knotted in a way only Caleb had patience for, the stack of notebooks with rubber bands that had given up their jobs.

She sliced a band with her thumbnail and opened a notebook on the bed. Caleb's handwriting looked like it had been in a hurry to become a person. Verses in the margins. Names of men with arrows to question marks. A line underlined twice: *Who benefits when we hush?*

Another page: a list titled **Paybacks**. Not money—acts. Fix Ms. Oates' porch. Drive Lydia to work (again). Bring Mama flowers (wild/cheap). Under that, a sentence: *If I die, remember it wasn't because I shouted. It was because they wouldn't listen.*

Naomi pressed her palm to the ink. The page remained unchanged and did not change.

The floor creaked. Evelyn stood in the doorway with a shoebox hugged to her chest. "I kept these because throwing them away felt like murder," she said. "And because keeping them felt like a crime."

"What are they?" Naomi asked.

"Pictures. Letters. A note from your father, I never answered." Evelyn set the box on the bed. The top photo was a Polaroid of three men in front of a truck. Paul was younger, his father's jaw wearing his smile. Beside him, Grandpa with his Sunday hand on a weekday shoulder. In the corner, a date blurred into light.

Under the photo, an envelope had browned to the color of tea—a bank letterhead. *Temporary extension approved contingent on cooperation with community development initiatives.* At the bottom, a loopy P. No last name. It didn't need one.

"My father said, 'Don't make trouble,'" Evelyn whispered. "I said it to myself so many times it felt like scripture. Your father fell in line. I… lined us behind him."

Naomi's voice was careful. "You think Dad owed Paul."

"I think we all owed somebody," Evelyn said. "Owing is this town's other public utility."

They looked at the paper until it began to look back at them.

"I'm taking this Tuesday," Naomi said.

"You can't," Evelyn said, reflex more than conviction.

"Then I'll memorize it and say it out loud," Naomi said, and felt the ghost of Caleb grin.

On the sidewalk by Bernice's house, Naomi didn't intend to stop. Voices through a cracked window made the decision for her.

"We're not going," Bernice said, vinegar-calm.

"We?" Tess's voice, bright and sharp. "You mean *me*. You mean no one makes a choice you didn't pick first?"

"Watch it," Joe warned, and the warning was sober, which made it more dangerous. "Paul's been good to us."

"Paul's been good to Paul," Tess snapped. "And to his list."

Micah's voice came low. "I'll stand in the back. Nobody has to see me."

"They'll see you," Bernice said, tired beyond anger. "They see all of us when they look at one of us. That's what family is in this town."

Silence pulled up a chair. Naomi pictured the rag. She pictured it *not* being wrung.

"Naomi's going to ruin us," Bernice said in a voice that had changed its mind twice on the way out.

"Or save us," Micah murmured.

Naomi stepped back before her shadow told on her. She counted to eight with her breath like Ruth had taught—a trick for when your body tries to outrun your mouth. When she turned, two girls on bikes swerved close and then wobbled, not from malice but from nerves. Naomi lifted a hand. They didn't wave back, but they also didn't laugh. Small mercies count.

The library had air-conditioning that acted as if it had paid for the building. Naomi walked the stacks to the microfilm machine like a person who had spent adolescence inside books when the world outside got loud. Ms. Calloway, who had laminated half of Millstone's childhoods, flicked the switch, and the machine growled awake.

"What are we hunting?" Ms. Calloway asked, as if gossip were a species the library collected.

"Old council minutes," Naomi said. "Community development initiatives. Who voted present and who 'had to step out.'"

"Won't find 'Paul' written plain," Ms. Calloway warned, not unkind. "You'll find initials and 'anonymous donor' and 'unexpected generosity.' But you can read where the ink smudges."

Naomi scrolled. Lines blurred into each other, then sharpened. *Roof repair funded. Clinic samples reallocated. Scholarship rescinded.* Names are missing where names should be. She took notes like a person tracing the outline of a thing they'd finally let themselves admit was there.

On her way out, Ms. Calloway slid a manila folder across the desk. "Newspaper from the year Caleb…," she said, stopping before the word. "There's a letter to the editor we didn't print. I keep the ones that told the truth at the wrong time."

Naomi didn't open it until she reached the steps. A typed page. No signature. *We are confusing quiet with peace. We are calling obedience wisdom. One day, we will have to tell our children why we asked them to shrink. I won't sign this because I am not brave enough to risk losing my job. But I am brave enough to say it to someone*—the date: one week before Caleb died.

She folded it twice, slid it into her bag like a future.

———————————————————————————

At dusk, Tess stood at the fence with her jaw set. "You love digging up bones," she said without greeting. "You'll bury us twice."

"I'm not digging," Naomi said. "I'm pointing to the bones people tripped over and pretended were roots."

"You keep saying Caleb's name like it unlocks something," Tess flared. "All it unlocks is more grief."

Micah hovered behind her, hands in pockets, eyes not hiding. "Grief and truth arrived together last time," he said. "Maybe this time they leave together, too."

Tess blew air through her nose like a horse choosing not to kick. "You think you're better."

"I think we can be better," Naomi said. "That's the difference."

Tess shook her head, braid slashing punctuation into the evening. "You'll see," she said and walked. Micah lingered.

"I found one of his notebooks once," he said, not looking at her. "Caleb's. He'd written, *If you can't stand up, sit up. If you can't sit up, speak up. If you can't speak, breathe like you mean it.*' I didn't understand then."

"And now?"

"I'm standing by degrees." He glanced up, gave her a thin, honest smile, then followed his sister at a pace that said he wasn't done being his own person.

Naomi stayed at the fence until the porch light came on by itself, as if the house had decided it would no longer wait to be asked.

Back at the table, Evelyn set the Polaroid on the wood, then the bank letter, then the envelope. The objects looked ordinary enough to pass as trash. Naomi knew better.

"Do you remember the night before he died?" Evelyn asked, not looking up.

Naomi did not say no. That word would have made her a liar twice.

"He told me he was going to write a speech," Evelyn said. "He said he'd say it even if nobody let him finish. I told him life isn't for speeches, it's for getting along." Her voice cracked. "I told him that because I was tired. I said hush because my bones rattled with the fear of a fight I had already lost."

Naomi put her hand over her mother's. "We lost that one," she said. "We don't have to lose the next."

Evelyn nodded, almost imperceptibly. "I'll bring the dress tomorrow to the cleaners," she said. "Blue looks better when it's bold."

Naomi smiled. "Blue looks good when it's honest."

They sat with the ghosts until the ghosts learned their place—to witness, not to rule.

CHAPTER 12

The Gentle Whisper

The storm broke at 3 a.m., cutting the sky into strips and sewing it back with thunder. Naomi sat up and waited for the old choreography—the rag twisting, the three-knock rhythm, the house making itself small. None of it came. Evelyn slept on, breath steady. The new choreography was quieter.

Naomi went outside barefoot. Rain soaked her shirt until it clung; her hair wrote commas down her neck. She stood on the porch and then left it, stepped into the yard as if stepping into a baptism nobody had scheduled.

Lightning stitched a last bright seam and then stopped. The rain thinned to a hush. Then even the hush ended.

Silence pushed into her ears like two warm hands. In it, a breeze curled around her calves and climbed—gentle as a whisper that had been patient for years. No words. Presence.

Elijah had looked for God in spectacle. The voice came in a still, small thing.

Naomi closed her eyes and heard it, where hearing doesn't have ears: 'You are not alone.' *You were never alone.* The sentence didn't answer anything, yet it somehow addressed what mattered. She sank to her knees, her palms in the wet grass, and let the earth cool her bones.

Dawn came in on its toes. Naomi shivered on the porch steps and gazed out at the street. Evelyn handed her coffee without ceremony.

"You were out in the rain," Evelyn said.

"Yes."

"Did it say anything back?"

"Yes," Naomi said. "But it didn't use words."

Evelyn considered that like a woman who had lived on sentences and was only now trying soup. "Hold onto it," she said quietly. "We'll need it."

They drank in companionable silence. The phone rang, and it didn't matter. It rang again and mattered less.

On errands, Naomi kept tripping over small, human things that felt like notes that had been slid under a door. At Mason's Market, the cashier with a braid too tight slid a receipt across the counter with three letters inked in the margin: *M.O.* Ms. Oates. Naomi turned. The older woman stood by the blood oranges like you could buy courage by the pound.

"You still fixing porches?" Naomi asked when she got close.

"I'm still needing 'em fixed," Ms. Oates said. "You coming Tuesday?"

"I am."

"I'll sit by the aisle so I can stand easily," Ms. Oates said. "And if my knees hold, I'll say my boy's name. They laid him off for saying no to a favor. Been calling it a budget cut ever since. I've budgeted my breath for this week." She patted Naomi's arm, bones and steel under thin skin. "Don't let me waste it."

At the pharmacy, Tess breezed past with her chin high and fear behind it. She didn't look at Naomi. Micah did, briefly, and tilted his head an eighth of an inch—the kind of nod a man gives when he's not ready to risk more in public.

Outside the hardware store, a boy wrestling a bike chain swore under his breath in a way that would keep his mama's hands busy later. Naomi crouched. "Mind if I help?" They worked in silence until the chain slid onto the sprocket like it had never considered rebellion. "Thank you," the boy muttered, embarrassed by gratitude. "My granddad says some problems don't want an audience." Naomi smiled. "Some problems need a witness." He considered that like a riddle and pedaled away.

At the far edge of town, the creek made its slow case for patience. Naomi stood on the footbridge and watched a leaf learn how to surrender without drowning. The air smelled like iron and green. She let the quiet in.

Ruth and Angel arrived with a rustle of paper and the thump of intention. Ruth set muffins down—the blueberry kind that never lasted an hour. Angel slapped a legal pad on the table and drew a line like a sword.

"Two-minute cap," Angel said. "So we practice two minutes that weigh a lifetime."

Ruth slid a list across. "Order of speakers," she said, neat as a choir roster. "You're in the first three, so nobody can close early without looking like cowards."

They drilled. Angel interrupted with heckles—"What do you have against unity?" "You just like attention."—and Naomi answered without running hot. Ruth called out time like a metronome that loved them.

Between rounds, Evelyn walked in and out in her blue dress, trying it on with and without a cardigan, with a brooch that made her neck look like a decision. "Too much?" she asked.

"Just enough," Ruth said. "You're not hiding at a funeral; you're attending a birth."

Angel grinned. "The birth certificate's going to have your signature on it, Evelyn."

Evelyn looked at herself in the microwave door and didn't flinch. "I'll sit in the front," she said. "If my hands shake, I'll let them. People need to see what bravery looks like with nerves."

They practiced until Naomi's voice warmed into something that didn't crack on the important words. When they finished, the kitchen felt taller by an inch.

In the afternoon, Naomi walked the boundary of places that had made her—schoolyard fence with initials carved into it like vows; the empty lot where Mr. Bentlee's feed store used to be before everybody pretended it never had a health inspection; the church where the marquee still clacked its reminder, LISTENING LISTENING LISTENING, like a tongue practicing an honest word.

At the council building, the janitor propped the door with his hip and nodded to her with the respect labor gives to courage, even when it hasn't joined it yet. Inside, the microphone waited on a stand that looked too thin for what it would have to hold.

Naomi stood in the doorway and pictured the room full—Ruth like a tree, Angel like a lit match, Evelyn in her blue dress like a flag they had learned to carry together. She pictured Paul's smile and did not rehearse a fight. She rehearsed a sentence she wanted to say as if it were a blessing, even when it cut.

She wrote it down on a torn corner of paper and folded it into her palm: *If unity needs my silence to survive, let it die and be reborn as something honest.*

Dusk made the streetlights remember themselves. On the porch, Evelyn had the phone on speaker again. "I'm asking you not to make a scene," Bernice said, voice more tired than mean. "You know how it goes when women get loud."

"I know how it goes when men do," Evelyn said. "We're trying the other way."

Bernice sighed. "My children live in my house."

"And mine lives in mine," Evelyn said. "Tomorrow she'll speak in front of yours."

The line clicked. Somewhere across town, a woman who had learned to wring rags put one down and thought about picking it up again. Somewhere, she didn't.

Angel texted: **Night drive. You need anything?**
Naomi replied: **Pray with your headlights. That's enough.**
Angel: **It's never enough. But okay.**

Ruth's message came like a benediction: **Sleep. Your words are already standing. You just need to join them.**

Naomi held the folded sentence in her hand and felt it soften with sweat. She opened the notebook and wrote more, not because she needed the lines but because writing is how some people breathe all the way out.

The world expects thunder. I will answer with a whisper that cuts stone. I will say my name first so that no one else claims it for me. I will say Caleb's next, so grief knows it has to share the room with hope. I will say Paul's without trembling, so power learns how to be looked at. And when the timer beeps, I will stop talking and keep speaking in the way I stand.

She closed the book. The house settled around the sentence like it had been waiting to hear it.

Night gathered its pieces. A moth battered itself against the porch light, insistent and ridiculous and holy in the way persistence always is. Across the street, Micah sat on his stoop with his elbows on his knees and stared at the place where tomorrow would happen. He lifted a hand, or maybe Naomi imagined it. Either way, it meant the same thing.

Inside, Evelyn laid the blue dress over a chair like a prayer cloth and turned off the lamp. Silence filled the house. It did not hush them. It held them.

Tomorrow, they would ask their mouths to do new work. Tonight, the whisper was enough.

CHAPTER 13

Broken,
But
Breathing

Part 1

The storm had rinsed the streets, but Naomi LeBlanc woke with her chest still heavy, as though thunder had left its weight in her ribs. She sat up slowly, listening for the old choreography—Evelyn's rag twisting, the three knocks on the kitchen table, a sigh that bent a room in half. None came.

Evelyn moved into the kitchen, humming low, the tune wobbly but real. Naomi padded barefoot down the hall and found her mother smoothing the blue dress across the chair back, pressing its wrinkles with reverence.

"You're wearing it?" Naomi asked.

Evelyn nodded. "Every day until Tuesday. If they're going to stare, let them stare at the truth."

Naomi poured herself a cup of coffee and leaned against the counter. The smell of chicory and damp wood made the morning feel older than it was. "Blue looks good when it's brave," she said.

Evelyn didn't smile, but her hands stopped trembling.

At Mason's Market, Naomi felt the eyes before she heard the words. Shelves lined with canned peaches and dry goods became pews, the customers an audience. She picked up bread, coffee, and a jar of jam.

"That's her," a voice whispered near the potatoes.
"Caleb's sister."
"Caleb's ghost."
"She'll burn the town if she's not careful."
"Maybe it needs burning."

Naomi's pulse kept time with her steps. She set the basket on the counter.

Mrs. Talley rang her up, her hands shaking. "You look tired, child," she whispered, low enough that only Naomi could hear. "Keep going. Sometimes the tired ones change more than the strong."

Naomi blinked fast, refusing to let the tears come. "Thank you."

Behind her, someone coughed. Another voice muttered, "LeBlancs never knew when to hush."

She walked out carrying groceries and a weight heavier than bread.

The post office was worse. Naomi collected the week's envelopes, most of them bills or junk mail. One was different: no return address, her name printed in letters sharp as nails. She slid her finger under the flap and pulled out a single scrap of paper.

ENOUGH.

The ink bled through, pressed so hard it left grooves. She folded it once, tucked it in her bag, and walked out without breaking stride.

On the steps, Mrs. Talley again—this time with her own mail in hand. "We prayed for peace," she said softly. "Maybe God's answer is the truth."

Naomi met her eyes. "I hope so."

Behind them, a man muttered to his companion, "Truth gets people killed."

Naomi didn't turn around.

At the pharmacy, Tess was at the counter, hair pulled back tight, ordering aspirin for Bernice. She caught sight of Naomi and her mouth curled.

"Still playing prophet?" Tess asked, loud enough for others to hear.

Naomi kept her voice calm. "Still playing shadow?"

Micah stepped out from behind the aisle, his hands in his pockets. His eyes darted between them, then settled on Naomi. He didn't speak, but the look was enough—half-apology, half-plea.

Tess snatched the bag from the counter and stormed past. "You'll get us all killed," she hissed as she brushed by.

Naomi stood still until the door slammed. Micah lingered, almost spoke, then followed his sister.

The barbershop was full of old men, their voices like sandpaper. Naomi slowed as she passed, the door cracked just enough to let the words spill.

"She's gonna stir trouble."
"Maybe trouble needs stirring."
"LeBlancs been trouble since her granddaddy knocked on tables."

Naomi walked on, but the words clung like burrs.

Part 2

That afternoon, Evelyn dragged a trunk from the hall closet, dust rising like ash. "I should have thrown this away years ago," she said, but her hands lingered on the latch.

Inside were letters yellowed to the color of tea, photographs curling at the edges, a child's report card, and a shoebox of receipts. Evelyn lifted one letter carefully. The handwriting was her father's: *Remember, the LeBlanc name survives if we don't make trouble.*

Naomi's throat tightened. "They thought silence was survival."

"They were wrong," Evelyn said, her voice flat.

Naomi picked up a Polaroid. Three men in front of a truck: Paul's father, her grandfather, and her own father, all smiles and handshakes. In the corner, the date blurred into light.

"They made bargains we never agreed to," Naomi whispered.

Evelyn looked away. "Bargains get passed down whether you agree or not."

Naomi set the photo back. "Then I'm breaking the chain."

She carried the weight of those letters to Ms. Oates' porch. The old woman sat in her rocker, bones thin but voice steady.

"You coming Tuesday?" Naomi asked.

Ms. Oates smiled faintly. "I've been waiting twenty years to say my boy's name. They fired him for refusing Paul's 'favor.' Called it a budget cut. Been lying ever since."

Naomi's chest ached. "Will you speak?"

"I'll sit by the aisle so I can stand easily," Ms. Oates said. "If my knees hold, I'll say his name. And if they don't, you say it for me."

Naomi nodded, eyes burning.

That evening, Ruth and Angel arrived, Ruth with a basket of cornbread, Angel with her boots scuffed and her mouth set in a sharp line.

"Two-minute cap," Angel said. "So we practice two minutes that weigh a lifetime."

Ruth nodded. "We'll drill. You speak, I'll time, Angel interrupts like the devil's advocate."

Naomi stood, words trembling at first. Angel heckled: "What do you have against unity? You just want attention."

Naomi's hands shook. She steadied her voice. "If unity means silence, then it isn't unity. It's control."

Ruth lifted her hand. "One minute left."

Naomi pressed on. "I will say my name first so no one owns it for me. I will say Caleb's name, so grief has to share the room with hope. I will say Paul's name without trembling, so power learns what it feels like to be looked at."

The timer buzzed. Naomi exhaled. Evelyn clapped softly from her chair, the blue dress across her lap.

"They'll hear you," Evelyn said. "Even if they don't want to."

Later that night, Naomi sat at her desk with Caleb's notebook open. His scrawl leapt from the page: *If you can't speak, breathe like you mean it.*

She closed her eyes and inhaled deeply, filling her lungs until they hurt. Broken, yes. But breathing.

She wrote in her own notebook: *We are cracked, but the cracks let the breath in. Broken, but breathing. That will be enough.*

The house creaked as if it agreed.

CHAPTER 14

Bloodlines
and
Bargains

The porch sagged under the weight of voices. Bernice's house had always been a gathering place for family—birthdays, funerals, Sunday dinners where someone brought macaroni salad and someone else brought secrets. But today, the air was thick with something that didn't taste like family at all.

Naomi paused at the gate, listening.

"...Paul kept this family fed," Joe said, voice already loud with indignation. "Paid the bills when nobody else would. You want to spit on that?"

Bernice's chair creaked. "He didn't feed us, Joseph. He fed on us. He gave with one hand and took with the other."

Tess snapped, sharp as a broken bottle. "That's not feeding. That's starving us slowly."

Naomi climbed the porch steps, her presence pulling their eyes. Micah saw her first, his elbows resting on his knees, gaze steady and unreadable.

Joe's lip curled. "Well, look who it is. Naomi LeBlanc. Come to add more poison?"

Naomi kept her voice even. "I didn't come to your porch. Your porch came to me. Your voices are louder than you think."

Joe stood, beer bottle swinging like punctuation. "Your daddy leaned on Paul, same as the rest of us. Don't you forget the LeBlanc name was bought and sold like cattle."

The words cut deeper than Joe knew. Naomi saw it—the envelope sliding across her father's table when she was twelve, Paul's father smiling like a banker counting coins, her father's hand trembling as he took it. A bargain made in silence, sealed with shame.

She inhaled, forcing herself back into the present. "Maybe he did. But I don't owe Paul for his bargains. Not one bit."

Tess stood, fists balled tight. "Neither do we."

Bernice slapped the arm of her chair. "We do. Don't lie to yourselves. This family's been kept alive by favors. You think houses get fixed, jobs get kept, bills get erased out of kindness? No, they get erased because Paul erased them. And now you want to stand up and pretend we're free?"

Naomi stepped closer. "Better broken than chained. If silence kept us alive, then what kind of living was it?"

Micah lifted his head, his voice low but certain. "If we're family, then tell me—do we inherit the bargains, or do we inherit the chains?"

The silence that followed was heavier than Joe's bottle slamming against the railing.

Later, Naomi sat with Evelyn at the kitchen table. The air smelled of coffee grounds and old wood, the kind of smell that clings to houses with too much history. Evelyn rubbed the hem of her dress between her fingers.

"I remember your father at Paul's table," Evelyn said quietly. "I told myself it was survival. We had mouths to feed. He took the envelope because I had begged him not to leave us without it. And every time I told him to hush, I was really telling myself."

Naomi swallowed. "Did you know what was inside?"

"Promises," Evelyn said. "Promises that tasted like chains. Money. Favors. Assurance that Caleb could keep his job one more season if we kept our mouths closed. Assurance that we wouldn't lose the house if we stopped asking questions."

Naomi's chest tightened. "And what did it cost?"

Evelyn met her eyes. "Your father. Caleb. Maybe me. Maybe you, if we're not careful."

Naomi touched her mother's hand. "It ends with me. I won't pass down silence like an heirloom."

The next morning, Naomi walked Main Street. Every porch had a story to tell, and none of them stayed quiet anymore.

"She thinks she's different."
"She'll drag the whole LeBlanc name through the dirt."
"Maybe that's what it needs."

She passed the diner. Loretta leaned out with a coffee pot in her hand. "You're making them nervous, Naomi," she said, voice low but fierce. "Keep it up."

At Mason's Market, the shopkeeper hesitated before taking her money. "You'd better be careful," he muttered. "People who owe Paul don't like being reminded they're debtors."

"I don't owe him," Naomi said firmly. "And I won't pay with silence."

Behind her, a man spat on the ground.

That afternoon, she stopped by the library. Ms. Calloway had a manila folder waiting. "Old letters," she explained. "Things that never made it into the paper. Thought you might want to see what courage looked like before it was fashionable."

Inside were letters from townsfolk who had once tried to speak. One read: *We are confusing quiet with peace. We call obedience wisdom. One day we'll have to tell our children why we asked them to shrink.*

No signature. Just fear. Naomi folded it carefully and slid it into her notebook.

As evening fell, Naomi walked past the church. The marquee clacked in the wind: **LISTENING SESSION TUESDAY.** The letters trembled but held.

Her footsteps echoed, and she imagined her father walking beside her, Caleb just behind, the weight of bargains pressing in. But this time she didn't bow. She squared her shoulders, breathing deep.

At home, she opened Caleb's notebook. His words jumped from the page: *Debt is silence wearing numbers. Break the silence, the debt dies.*

She pressed her hand against the ink, whispering, "I hear you."

Then she wrote her own vow:

The bargains end with me. I will not carry them. I will not pass them down. If silence is our inheritance, then I am disowning it. My name is Naomi LeBlanc, and I am not for sale.

She set the pen down, exhaled, and felt her lungs fill again. Broken, yes. But breathing.

CHAPTER 15

A Town
of
Watchers

The town had eyes. Not just the kind that glanced over fences or peeked through curtains, but eyes that lingered, measured, judged. Millstone had always been a town of porches, and porches meant watchers.

Naomi felt them everywhere.

At first, it was subtle—blinds tilted just so, lace curtains trembling. Then it became bold: heads turned, conversations halted mid-sentence, whispers loud enough to be heard but quiet enough to be denied.

She walked Main Street, the soles of her shoes striking against the cracked pavement. Each step seemed to echo longer than it should have.

At the diner, Loretta slid her a cup of coffee before Naomi even asked. The pot hovered, steam curling in the morning light.

"You're making them nervous," Loretta said, her lipstick bright as war paint. "Keep it up."

The regulars at the counter went quiet. One cleared his throat. Another muttered, "Nervous turns to angry."

Loretta's eyes narrowed. "Angry doesn't scare me. Angry just proves they're listening."

Naomi sipped the coffee. It was stronger than usual, bitter enough to burn, and she let it.

Outside the barbershop, old men leaned on their canes, voices gruff as sandpaper.

"She's gonna stir trouble," one said.
"Maybe trouble needs stirring," another countered.

"LeBlancs been trouble since her granddaddy's knocks," the third muttered.

Naomi didn't break stride, but their words clung to her like burrs.

Children played ball in the street. A boy shouted, "Don't end up like Caleb!" His mother's hand flew to hush him, face red with shame, but Naomi had already heard.

Another boy, younger, watched Naomi with wide eyes. He didn't laugh, didn't jeer. Just looked at her like she was something he didn't yet have a word for.

Naomi gave him the slightest nod. He didn't nod back, but he didn't look away either.

At the churchyard, Sister May arranged flowers with delicate precision. She caught Naomi watching and pursed her lips.

"Unity, child," she said. "We need unity, not division."

Naomi held her gaze. "Unity without truth is just silence dressed up."

Sister May sniffed, placing a daisy with unnecessary force. "Silence keeps the peace."

"Peace built on silence isn't peace," Naomi answered.

Sister May didn't reply. The flowers trembled in her hands.

That afternoon, Ruth and Angel canvassed. Naomi joined them.

At one house, a woman opened the door just enough to listen. "I support you," she whispered. "But don't say my name. My husband…" She trailed off, eyes darting. "You understand."

The door slammed before Angel finished her sentence.

Angel kicked the step on the way down. "Cowards," she muttered.

Ruth laid a hand on her arm. "Fear isn't cowardice. It's captivity. They're still chained."

Angel scowled. "Chains don't break if you polish them."

Naomi said nothing. She knew both women were right.

Back at Evelyn's, Tess appeared on the porch, arms crossed tight.

"You're dragging us all down," Tess snapped.

Evelyn, steady in her blue dress, surprised them both. "Better down with truth than up with lies."

Tess flinched as if struck. Micah stood behind her, silent but present.

Naomi met Tess's glare. "Nobody's forcing you to come Tuesday."

"Maybe I'll come just to see you fall," Tess shot back, storming off.

Micah lingered, his eyes softer. He gave Naomi the faintest nod, then followed his sister.

Evening fell. Naomi sat on her porch with her notebook, the pages filled with Caleb's words, her own vows, scraps of courage collected from the day.

Across town, windows glowed. One by one, they flickered out, like eyes closing. But Naomi knew they weren't sleeping. Millstone was watching itself, waiting to see what Tuesday would bring.

The weight of those unseen eyes pressed on her chest. But she inhaled, slow and deep, steady. Broken, yes. But breathing.

The night hummed with anticipation. The town had chosen its role: it would watch. Whether as jury, executioner, or witness—that remained to be seen.

Naomi closed her notebook and whispered to the dark: "Then watch. I'm ready to be seen."

CHAPTER 16

The Listening Session

The council hall smelled like disinfectant and old plywood, a civic kind of sanctity. Rows of metal chairs faced a folding table with three microphones and a pitcher of water that sweated as if it were nervous too. A hand-lettered sign on the door read: LISTENING SESSION – TWO-MINUTE LIMIT – RESPECTFUL CONDUCT. Someone had underlined *respectful* three times, as if underlines could save a town.

The janitor pushed a broom down the center aisle, stopping to tug a leg until a wobbly chair agreed to stand straight. "Behave," he told the chair, and it did.

Ruth arrived first, steady as a bell, a leather notebook tucked under her arm. Angel came next, boots announcing themselves, eyes scanning corners like a soldier mapping exits. Loretta slipped in, wearing lipstick as bright as conviction, and sat where a woman could clap loudly without apology.

Evelyn stood in the doorway for one long breath. The blue dress made her look like a promise kept. Naomi took her mother's hand, and they walked in together. Heads turned. Conversations paused mid-syllable, the town's mouth remembering its manners in pieces.

Paul waited near the microphones, flanked by men who had learned how to fold their hands in a way that made them look reasonable. Reverend Carter hovered like a benediction the room hadn't earned; he wore concern the way some men wear cologne—liberally, hoping it covers what lingers beneath.

Bernice entered with Tess two steps ahead and Micah two steps behind. Joe came last, the smell of last night's choices clinging to him like a coat. Sister May's hat arrived five minutes before she did.

Ms. Oates shuffled down the aisle, found a seat at the end of a row, and patted the armrest as if it were a friend she trusted not to move. The nurse from the clinic sat near her, lips pressed thin over words that had been waiting a year.

The room filled until the air felt like a chest too small for the breath it needed to hold.

Paul tapped the microphone. "Thank you for coming," he began, voice practiced, benevolent. "We're here to listen. We're here for unity."

Angel's eyebrow climbed like a question. Ruth wrote *Unity ≠ hush* on her pad and drew a box around it.

The timer on the table glowed an impartial red.

"Two minutes per person," the councilman to Paul's right announced. "Speak your piece. Be respectful. No names."

A murmur rolled. Naomi felt the sentence buckle inside her—*no names*—and set it back upright with her will.

Paul smiled at the room like a man handing out hymnals. "Who'd like to begin?"

Silence hesitated, then stepped aside. Naomi stood.

Gasps stitched across the room. Evelyn's hand tightened around her daughter's for half a second and then let go, the way you release something you intend to bless.

Naomi walked to the microphone and adjusted it to her height. The timer blinked: 2:00.

"My name is Naomi LeBlanc," she said, clear and level, and the first gasp turned into an intake of breath the whole room shared. "I will say it first so no one owns it for me."

The timer dropped to 1:56.

"I am here to tell the truth we all live under," Naomi continued. "Our town confuses quiet with peace. We call obedience wisdom. We ask our children to shrink so the powerful don't have to. My brother, Caleb, tried to speak. You buried him in shame and called it unity."

A sound rose—part pain, part warning. Paul's smile thinned, but did not leave.

"At our clinic," Naomi went on, "samples are reallocated for the compliant. In our schools, scholarships appear and vanish depending on who's smiled at which table. In our homes, rags are twisted and tables knocked three times to keep questions from being born."

Sister May's hat dipped; Loretta's hands flattened on her knees. Evelyn's jaw trembled once and then was still.

"You asked us not to name names," Naomi said, "but silence is a person here. It has donors, deacons, and a ledger with initials. I brought a copy."

A hush ran sharply through the room. Naomi lifted a folded slip—penciled columns, cramped letters, that looping P at the bottom of a line like a flourish that wanted to be a signature without the courage.

Paul reached for his water and didn't drink. Reverend Carter's eyes dropped to his folded hands as if prayer might hide him.

"Debt is silence wearing numbers," Naomi said, voice steady as a plumb line. "Break the silence, the debt dies."

The timer flashed: 0:22.

"I will say my name first," she repeated, "Caleb's next—because grief must share the room with hope—and Paul's without trembling so power learns what it feels like to be looked at."

A ripple turned wave. Someone hissed. Someone clapped once, surprised at themselves. Angel stood without meaning to, pride lifting her like a tide.

The timer hit 0:00. Naomi did not race the beep. She stopped on the breath that felt right.

"Thank you," she said and stepped back.

"Two minutes," the councilman snapped, voice finding courage inside a rule.

"Two minutes can carry a lifetime," Ruth replied softly, not into a microphone, and somehow the room heard.

Paul leaned forward, fatherly. "We appreciate your passion, Miss LeBlanc. We're not here to accuse. We're here to heal."

"Truth heals," Naomi said, not into the mic, and sat.

Ms. Oates surprised the room by standing without help. She took the aisle seat, then the aisle, then the center.

"My son said no to a favor," she told the room, each word a board laid down, careful and sure. "They fired him. Called it a budget. Been lying ever since. His name is Reed Oates. I wanted you to hear a name and remember it belongs to a person."

"Names," the rule-man began, but his voice withered under the weight of Ms. Oates' eyes.

The nurse stood next. "We have rules for samples," she said, voice shaking but not failing. "And another set of rules for people with friends. I've been complicit. I'm sorry."

The janitor hovered near the back, hat in hand. He didn't come forward. He tilted his head toward Angel. She rose, walked to the mic, and held it for him from ten feet away.

He cleared his throat. "I sweep this room," he said. "I hear things fall under tables. I pick up paper people didn't mean to drop. I'm not brave. But I'm not blind."

He sat. Angel's grin was a weapon put back in its holster.

Tess walked to the center aisle and stalled. Her face flickered between fury and something that looked like grief before it knew how to cry. "You're tearing us in half," she told Naomi across the rows.

"Maybe we needed to be torn to grow," Naomi answered.

Bernice stood as if pulled by a string. "I told my children silence keeps us safe," she said. "I said it until it sounded like God. I was wrong."

Joe laughed, a sound that was ugly yet tried to be strong. "We're alive, aren't we?" he barked. "What's wrong with alive?"

"Alive isn't the same as living," Micah said, to no one and everyone.

Paul lifted both hands, palms open, a man surrendering to his own script. "Let's close in prayer," he said smoothly, sensing the swell and trying to time it.

"After we finish listening," Ruth said, mild on the surface, iron beneath.

"Two minutes each," the rule-man repeated, louder, insisting on order now that truth had learned to walk.

They kept coming. A teacher. A grocer. A boy who didn't speak, just held up a basketball with Caleb's name written in Sharpie and let the room see it. Sister May stepped to the microphone and said only, "Lord, have mercy," in a voice that did not tell the Lord which way to aim it.

When the swell dipped, Paul moved in. "Let me offer a prayer for unity," he said, and bowed his head, because men like him know how to win with their eyes closed.

"Unity that requires my silence may as well be a noose," Naomi said, not loud, not theatrical—just true. The words found their own volume.

Carter began praying anyway, a soft wash of scripture and safety. "Make us one," he said.

"Make us honest," Ruth said over him, eyes open.

"Make us brave," Angel added, grinning at the ceiling.

The hall held all three prayers at once, which is to say the hall finally told the truth about what it had been carrying for years.

When it seemed to end, it didn't. People stood and didn't leave. Groups formed, dissolved, reformed; plans were made in whispers that did not apologize. Ms. Oates sat and cried into a handkerchief that had seen five funerals and two weddings and one birth she thought might save them and hadn't yet. The nurse wrote down a date and handed it to Naomi—"When you call, I'll testify."

Bernice walked past Naomi without looking at her and wiped her cheeks like rain she could pretend away if she moved fast enough. Joe pushed through the doors as if the air outside might be less real.

Micah waited. When Naomi got to him, he said, "I'll stand next time," and she believed him.

Outside, the sun had not moved; it only looked like it had because the town had finally shifted. The marquee at Hope Chapel clacked in the wind. LISTEN… ING… as if the word itself had learned to breathe.

CHAPTER 17

Sides Are Chosen

By morning, Millstone had sorted itself into tribes the way small towns do when someone rearranges the furniture of truth. The difference was that this time the sorting happened in daylight.

Loretta taped a paper by the diner register: NO HARASSMENT. EAT OR LEAVE. Underneath, in smaller letters, *Iced tea refills are still free; act right.* Men read it with offense and then ordered anyway, because habit is stronger than pride at lunchtime.

Ms. Oates' porch was filled with casseroles that nobody had asked permission to bring. The nurse's mailbox held three envelopes with no return address, each containing a Bible verse and no threat, which in Millstone could be perceived as a threat if one tilted it wrong.

At the barber shop, Old Mr. Harris declared, "I ain't cutting hair for cowards," and three men pretended they needed to be somewhere else.

Sister May's hat was at the church early, flowers arranged with surgical care. She wrote *"UNITY" on the fellowship hall whiteboard and then, after staring at it, added "TRUTH" above it and circled both, creating* a Venn diagram drawn with hope.

Reverend Carter stood at his office window and watched the street. He practiced a sermon about peace, empathy, and not letting outsiders define their town, but then he discarded his first draft because it reeked of fear. He started over with Micah 6:8, and a tremor in his wrist he didn't want to admit to.

Paul held a meeting behind the closed door of the development office. Men leaned forward with their elbows on the table, the way men do when they plan to be persuasive. "We stay above reproach," Paul said. "We weather this. People forget. They always do." He said it like a blessing he had given before and had every intention of giving again.

Joe made a circuit of porches with warnings in his mouth and a hangover in his eyes. At Bernice's, he found Tess on the steps, jaw squared like a hinge tightened too far. "We ain't going to any more circuses," Joe told her.

Tess stared past him at the street. "We're already in the ring," she said. "We can at least learn to throw the right punches."

Micah hammered a sign into Ms. Oates' yard that read TUESDAY WASN'T THE LAST TIME and felt his spine straighten a fraction. When Bernice called him in for lunch, he left the hammer on the grass on purpose, a small defiance that made him feel like air had more room in it.

At Evelyn's, the blue dress hung on the back of a chair like a flag that had decided to be a garment when it needed to. Naomi flipped pancakes for breakfast because muscle memory sometimes saves a morning. Angel had slept on the couch to "guard the perimeter," which meant scaring off shadows with her snore. Ruth arrived with fruit and a prayer that didn't need to be said out loud to work.

"Someone called the house last night," Evelyn said over coffee. "Didn't speak. Just breathed like they wanted me to learn their lungs."

"What did you do?" Angel asked, already ready to fight a voice.

"I breathed back," Evelyn said. "Louder."

Naomi laughed, and the laugh sounded like it had been waiting its turn for months.

They spent the day walking. Not canvassing, not campaigning. Just moving through the town like a procession of ordinary. People watched. Some nodded. Some crossed streets. A child waved and then hid behind her mother's skirt and peeked out again, curious as light.

The nurse crossed the street holding a manila folder to her chest. "Copies," she said without preamble. "Of memos. Of 'exceptions granted.' I'm tired of apologizing for doing the right thing late." She looked smaller and bigger at the same time. "If they fire me, at least I'll stop washing dirt off my hands that I didn't put there."

Ruth took the folder and put it in her bag like a sacrament. "Thank you," she said, and meant it in the oldest sense of the word.

They stopped by the library. Ms. Calloway had a stack of microfilm spindles on the desk, labeled in pencil—COUNCIL 2001–2006, GRANTS / DONORS, LETTERS NOT PRINTED. "I can't tell you to look," she said, "and I can't tell you not to. But the machine's been tested and the bulb is fresh." She tapped the counter twice, an old librarian's blessing.

"Why help us?" Naomi asked.

Ms. Calloway gave a small, wry smile. "I like index cards. Truth is a kind of filing system. I've waited a long time to put this town in order."

By evening, lines had been drawn, erased, and redrawn. Some people posted Bible verses about unity with images of doves and then locked their doors. Others posted nothing and left their porch lights on later than usual, a code for *you to knock*.

A spray of paint appeared on the wall behind the post office: ENOUGH. It wasn't the same handwriting as the notes. This one looked like a prayer shouted.

Naomi stood in front of it, the word taller than she was. Angel chuckled. "Finally, graffiti I can get behind," she said.

They took the long way home. At a corner, Paul stepped from the doorway of his office like a man exiting a stage between acts.

"Miss Naomi LeBlanc," he said, cordial, each syllable measured to fill the space between them but not more. "A word."

Naomi stopped because running would have been its own kind of permission.

Paul's smile found its shape. "You're better at this than you think," he said. "You moved people last night. That's dangerous when you don't know where you're going."

"I know exactly where I'm going," Naomi said.

"Do you?" His voice softened, almost tender, the way a blade can feel smooth before it cuts. "Your family has eaten at my table. Your father understood exchange. Your mother understands it, too, though she dresses it now in blue."

Angel shifted—one step closer, one postcard of a snarl.

Paul's eyes flicked to her, then back to Naomi. "I don't want this to hurt you," he said. "Truly. We can course-correct. We can make amends. We can find a path that honors unity and spares your…reputation."

He reached into his pocket and produced a folded letter on thick paper. "A statement," he said. "A reframe. You spoke with passion. You do not accuse. You desire healing. We'll release it together."

Naomi didn't take the paper. "No."

Paul held it a moment longer, as if the letter might leap into her hand if he gave it time. When it didn't, he refolded it with neat corners. "Be careful," he said, a benediction curdled to a warning. "This town is small. Grace has limits."

"God doesn't," Ruth said, voice quiet, appearing on Naomi's other side like scripture when you need it and didn't memorize it in time.

Paul nodded once, not conceding, and returned to his doorway. "People forget," he said again, to the door more than to them.

"Not this time," Naomi answered, to the air.

They walked on. Behind them, the letter in Paul's pocket rustled as he slid it away, like paper unhappy to be folded.

CHAPTER 18

The Cost of Truth

Morning brought consequences with the mail.

A plain envelope featuring the development office letterhead, with a tone that attempted civility. **Notice of Concern**, it said, is anodyne language surrounding a threat: Statements made in public forums may expose parties to civil action if their *reputations are harmed*. It wasn't a lawsuit. It was a weather report for a storm somebody wanted to schedule.

Evelyn read it twice and placed it on the table. "We are not wealthy," she said in a voice that didn't apologize for the fact. "We can't fight in courts."

"We can fight in rooms," Naomi said. "And kitchens. And porches. And hearts. That's where he's been winning. That's where we win back."

"Also," Angel added, "we can fight in parking lots if absolutely necessary." Ruth didn't correct her out loud, which was its own kind of permission and made Angel grin.

At the diner, Loretta had company: a policeman in a pressed uniform who had decided virtue could be worn like a shirt. He spoke too loudly to a man who nodded too quickly. "We just want folks to be safe," the officer said, and wrote nothing down in a notebook with blank pages.

When Naomi walked in, he looked up, looked down, touched the brim of his hat as if that gesture could count as community service. "Ma'am," he said, and left.

"Coward," Loretta muttered, then brightened. "Honey, I tried a new biscuit recipe. If you say it's good, I'll name it after you. If you say it's bad, I'll still name it after you and call it satire."

The biscuits were flaky and stubborn—Angel's favorite kind of carbohydrate. Naomi ate and did not taste much, but was grateful anyway.

By noon, the first practical cost arrived. Ms. Oates' electric bill doubled, and the note at the bottom—**DELINQUENT**—was dated a week before it should have been. The nurse's schedule changed without warning; all her hours now fell between midnight and six a.m., a punishment disguised as opportunity. A boy in Naomi's neighborhood found his bike stolen and returned with its chain cut wrong, so it would grind and teach him a lesson.

"Tit for tat," Ruth said, calmly furious. "Small violences. They forget God counts those, too."

Naomi spent the afternoon calling people who had stood the night before. She did not offer comfort. She offered presence. "I'll drive you," she told the nurse. "I'll sit with you," she told Ms. Oates. "I'll replace it," she told the boy. "And I'll fix the chain right."

On the way home, a rock hit the porch rail—not hard enough to break, just hard enough to be heard. Naomi opened the door. The rock wore a paper band like a crown. *LEAVE*, printed in that same carved-hand scrawl.

Evelyn stepped onto the porch, took the rock, and placed it in a clay pot by the steps. "We're planting threats now," she said. "See if they bloom."

That evening, the phone rang. Bernice. "He's getting mean," she said without introduction, voice small. "Joe. He says you've made us targets. He says Paul has a list. I've always known he had one." Her voice cracked. "I don't want my children on it."

"They're already on it," Naomi said gently. "So are we. That's why we're doing this out loud. Lists hate sunlight."

Bernice inhaled like a woman learning how to. "I can bring food," she said, defaulting to the language she knew. "I can sit next to you and not leave, even if I shake."

"That is more than enough," Naomi said, and meant it.

Darkness arrived early, the way it does when a town is tired of itself. The porch light drew moths; their wings made a sound like paper being forgiven. Micah sat on his stoop across the street and raised a hand in a hello that was also a vow.

They met at Ruth's after nightfall. The kitchen table had acquired a map—a hand-sketched plan of where people would stand next week, who would speak first, where the elderly would sit with the best lines of sight, and the shortest route to the aisle.

"I talked to the janitor," Angel said. "He can't stand at a microphone. But he'll place a folder under the third chair from the left in the front row. Inside: copies. Ledger pages. Names blacked out, initials not. We'll let the town do its own math."

Ruth added a verse to the margin of the map—Proverbs, about honest scales, about balances that please the Lord. "Not because we need a verse to be right," she said, "but because it steadies my hands to remember He cares about weights and measures more than any council ever did."

Evelyn came late, hair damp from a shower that hadn't washed away fear but had at least put it in clean clothes. She sat without asking where; the chair knew her.

"They sent a letter," she told them, laying *Notice of Concern* on the table like a charge she was entering into evidence. "I don't know how to fight paper."

"Paper fought us first," Naomi said. She tapped the map, the verse, the ledger copy, then her notebook, and finally the manila folder from the nurse. "We'll use paper, too."

Angel's grin went feral. "Weaponize stationery," she said. "I like it."

They planned until the clock stopped. When they rose, Ruth prayed the kind of prayer you can tuck into a pocket and find later when your hands need something to do besides tremble.

On the porch, the night was the same night it had been the day before. The difference was that the town had learned to hear itself breathing.

Before sleep, Naomi opened Caleb's notebook. *If you can't stand up, sit up. If you can't sit up, speak up. If you can't speak, breathe like you mean it.* She wrote underneath in her smaller hand: *We are standing. When we sit, we will still be tall. When we speak, we will remember our breath belongs to us.*

She closed the book and set it on the chair where she'd see it when she woke.

Far down the block, a car idled, moved, idled again—caution disguised as routine. A porch light blinked out. Another flickered on. Somewhere, a dog barked at a thing it could not name and then lay down with a sigh that said it loved its people anyway.

The cost had begun to tally up. The ledger this time would not be kept by the men with the comfortable pens.

When Naomi turned off her lamp, the room did not go dark. It held the faint light of a town that had started counting differently.

ACT III

The Reckoning

CHAPTER
19

Still Becoming

The rock in the clay pot wore last night's dew like a crown that didn't belong to it. The paper band around it—*LEAVE*—had soaked and wrinkled, but the letters still pressed through like a bruise. Naomi stood on the porch with her coffee and watched the street breathe in slow, suspicious lungs. Somewhere, a screen door banged; somewhere else, a radio tried to be cheerful and failed.

Evelyn stepped out, robe tied, hair pinned with the practical mercy of a woman who intends to get through a day. She lifted the rock and set it back down. "Do we throw it out?"

"No," Naomi said. "We keep it where they can see we saw it."

Evelyn nodded, then looked at the flowerbed. "Or we plant it deeper." She dug two fingers into the damp soil at the border, pressed the rock in until only the crown showed. "Let people learn what threats grow into." She dusted her hands. "Nothing."

By mid-morning, the town answered in its oldest dialect: petty punishments spoken like policy.

At Ms. Oates's house, the electricity snapped off just as her kettle began to whisper. She stood in the kitchen with her hand wrapped in the cord like a leash she refused to hold. "Paid already," she muttered, showing Naomi the receipt. "Dated last week." She folded the paper once, then again, then slipped it under the magnet that held up Reed's graduation photo. "They can have the light," she said, rocking. "But not my boy's name."

At the clinic, the nurse walked in to find her schedule blank. "We'll call you," the manager said with a smile he'd practiced for years. "Budget constraints." In the hallway, two mothers called after her, "We'll wait for you." The nurse pressed her lips together until they whitened and whispered to Naomi, "I'm tired of apologizing for doing the right thing late."

At the library, the glass case that had held the "community archive" sat open and empty, the lock still latched to nothing. "Moved for inventory," read a Post-it in handwriting that tried to be casual. Ms. Calloway stared at it like a woman whose family Bible had gone missing and been replaced by a brochure. "Truth does not check itself out," she said, pinching the note off with two fingers, "and it does not return late."

On the sidewalk, two boys chalked a hopscotch grid. One had drawn a square labeled **JUMP** between numbers six and seven. The other shook his head. "It's not how you play," he said. "It is now," the first answered without looking up.

Threats moved indoors when the sun climbed.

The phone rang at Evelyn's, and when she answered, no word came— only a long inhale, then a longer hold, then a click. Naomi watched Evelyn set the receiver down, pick it up, set it down again. The third time, Evelyn hit the speaker and put the cordless phone in the middle of the table as evidence.

When the call returned, Naomi spoke first. "Say what you came to say."

Breath. A low voice at last. "For your safety," it said. She recognized the officer's cadence, the way authority sounds when it wants credit for concern. "For the town's peace."

"Order without justice is furniture," Evelyn said, eyes on the blue dish towel she refused to twist. "It sits. It does not save."

The line cut. Angel pushed through the door a minute later, boots clapping the tile. "They keyed my car," she announced, grin sharp. "Right along the driver's side. Wrote **HUSH** with a nail like poetry gone wrong." She flopped into a chair. "Good news? I parked where the camera at the bakery sees everything except my good side."

Ruth arrived with a pie and a list, set both down as if the table had been waiting for their weight. "We'll catalog every incident. Times. Places. Names if we have them, habits if we don't." She looked at Naomi. "Fear is trying to make you smaller. We will not assist it."

Naomi laughed once, a sound too bright to be exactly happy. "I almost said maybe we should leave," she admitted to the wood grain. "Just for a second. The thought came like a cat at the screen, pawing."

"Leave?" Angel snorted. "And teach them the strategy works? Hard pass."

Ruth slid her a pen. "Write the thought down. Thoughts lose some teeth on paper."

Naomi wrote: *Leave.* Then, beneath it, slower: *Stay.* She drew a square around the second word and shaded the square until it felt like a floor.

She tried to nap, but she dreamed of Caleb anyway. He stood at the edge of a plain of tall grass, wind pushing it in long exhales. He held his notebook out to her, open to a page she'd never seen: *If truth hurts you, it means you are healing in a place where lies grew like callus.* He smiled that old, lopsided smile that had made teachers forgive deadlines and made Paul's men hate him for reminding them they still had souls.

When she woke, the room was filled with lighter air. She carried the notebook to the porch and set it beside the clay pot. The sun had dried the paper crown stiff on the first rock. Naomi peeled it off, slid it into the back pocket of Caleb's book, and wrote under his line: *Hurt is not the same as harm. We are sore, not slain.*

Across the street, Micah sat on the steps with a hammer in his lap and no nails. He lifted it in a half salute. Tess stood behind the screen door, arms crossed, mouth a hard line that looked less like hatred and more like a woman holding her fear where it couldn't fly at the wrong person.

Bernice called from inside for the third time that day, "Lunch," and for the first time all week, her voice didn't break on the final syllable.

Evening changed costume and brought cruelty dressed as clever.

A mason jar shattered on Naomi's porch rail, and milk slid down the wood in slow white tears. Inside the shards, someone had stuffed a soggy strip of paper that read *SPILL AGAIN*. Evelyn swept glass as if she were making a bed. "Creative is just cowardice with craft supplies," she said, not unkindly. She swept until the wood gleamed. Then she laid a dish towel over the rail, the good one, the blue one, a banner reclaimed.

In the window across the street, a shadow lifted a phone and lowered it. In the next house over, a dog barked at the air and then decided to love it.

Naomi set the broom aside and called Ruth; called Angel; called the nurse; called Ms. Oates; called Ms. Calloway. She did not offer comfort. She offered presence. "I'll replace your groceries," she told Ms. Oates. "I'll sit with you for the night," she told the nurse. "I'll bring a flashlight," she told Ms. Calloway. "We don't do alone anymore," she told all of them.

Before she went to bed, she planted each new rock halfway into the soil beside the first. Evelyn labeled the little graveyard with a wooden spoon, the handle stuck firmly into the ground. On the spoon, she printed with a laundry marker: **MUSEUM OF FAILED IDEAS.**

They stood together to admire the sign. "Field trips on Wednesdays," Angel said.

"Bring your own breath," Ruth added.

They laughed, and the sound was the kind that teaches nights not to be so proud of themselves.

The next morning, the clay pot was gone. In its place, a smaller stone held down a torn piece of grocery bag on which someone had scrawled **LAST CHANCE**. Naomi held it up to the sun so the holes in the paper could show her the sky. "Then let this be the last chance to back down," she said. "Missed."

Evelyn smoothed the robe and exchanged it for the blue dress without flinching. "Then this is our first chance to continue."

They stood and did, breathing in the way Caleb had taught her, the way Ruth had named, the way Angel had defended, the way Evelyn had found again.

Broken, yes. But breathing. And that made silence tremble.

CHAPTER
20

Rooted in Ashes

The breaking glass woke the birds before it woke Naomi. When she sat up, the sound had already gone elsewhere, but the feeling remained: a vibration in the air like a string plucked and allowed to waver until it found its own end.

On the porch, a mason jar had exploded into constellations. Milk slicked the boards like an attempted baptism. The paper inside dripped letters: *SPILL AGAIN*. If the town wanted a metaphor, it was supplying its own.

Evelyn swept as if sweeping could save the world if you did it long enough. "Jars instead of mouths," she said. "Notes instead of names. Boys throwing stones from the backs of men."

Naomi knelt, gathered a shard between forefinger and thumb. The blue dish towel fluttered, unafraid. "Every jar proves the point," she said. "The quiet has always been enforced."

"Then we enforce something else," Evelyn said, and her broom kept time with her words.

Mason's Market was all theater: aisles like aisles, but stages if you listened. When Naomi stepped in, conversations learned to pretend they had other things to do. A man in a ball cap—Frank, who had three opinions about sports and two about women who spoke—muttered "troublemaker" as if testing the weight of the word on his tongue.

The clerk, Danny, looked everywhere but at her face. "Your card may not run," he warned, shame flushing his neck like a kid caught cheating at checkers.

"Then I'll use cash," Naomi said. "Truth spends better." She laid bills on the mat like dignity.

Frank laughed, then coughed to make it sound like an accident. Loretta materialized by the freezer case, holding coffee filters and a gaze that could freeze a pie at ten paces. "She's not asking for trouble," Loretta said to the room without tilting her chin. "You keep handing it out."

A can of peaches toppled off a shelf in an aisle and clanged onto the floor like a period in a sentence God intended to keep.

By noon, rumor had replaced weather as the town's favorite topic.

"She's getting sued."

"She's leaving town by Friday."

"Paul's got friends in Nashville and cousins in the courthouse."

"She's cursed."

"She's a prophet."

At the barbershop, men lifted their voices as Naomi passed, much like peacocks lift their feathers to show color and hide fear. "A LeBlanc never knew when to quit," one said. "Look where it got Caleb."

Naomi paused, turning so they wouldn't have to waste energy speaking to each other. "Remembered," she said. "And remembered is stronger than forgotten." She walked on before the reply could find its way from throat to mouth.

Outside the post office, someone had taken chalk to the brick again. Over the fading **ENOUGH**, a new hand had written **AGAIN**. The word looked less angry than determined.

They met at Ruth's table because, in times of chaos, tables are what keep people at the same height.

Maps. Notes. Photos of the clay pot museum. A list of doors that needed escorts, a list of porches that would accept bread, a list of men who had learned to listen so recently they needed practice.

"They're escalating," Angel said. "Which means they're scared. Which means they're sloppy. Which means we can catch them looking like themselves."

Ruth set her pen down and folded her hands. "We can't just catch. We have to care." She looked at Naomi. "How's your heart?"

"Humming too high," Naomi said. "Like a machine that thinks fast will win, even if it burns out."

Ruth nodded as if Naomi had turned in a form on time. "Then we go slower in the middle. Slowness is a weapon they never trained for."

"Logistics," Angel translated, smirking.

"Love," Ruth corrected.

"Same letters," Angel said. "Different order."

They all smiled, then set to assigning walks like relatives distributing casseroles after a funeral—competently, with tenderness.

The breaking point was found through Tess.

She burst onto the porch at speed, hair half out of its tie, breath coming in strips. "They cornered Micah after school," she said, not so much greeting as siren. "Three boys. Big. Seniors. Said if he keeps standing next to you, he won't stand at all."

Angel stood before the verb had finished. "Names."

Tess swallowed hard. "I don't—" She did. She said them. They sounded like wood you'd never noticed creaking until you tried to sleep.

Naomi put a hand out—not to stop Angel, not to unleash her, but to place herself between action and reaction like a resistor in a circuit. "We walk him home. Today, tomorrow, the next. We make it normal to stand near me until it's normal to stand near the truth."

Tess paced three steps and back. "I can't lose him," she said, voice a thin wire. "I was mad at you for making him brave. Then I realized you just named the brave he already had."

"Brave is not a thing we make people eat," Ruth said. "It's a word we put next to them so they can see themselves when they're shaking."

Angel cracked her knuckles, not unkindly. "I like 'shaking brave.' That's my genre."

"Thank you," Tess said, to all of them at once, a sentence some women don't know how to say until they do, and then they can't stop.

They did not call the police because the police had already asked them to be silent. They called the janitor. He stood in the hallway at the school with his cart like a general who had traded medals for mops. "Camera by the cafeteria picks up the edge of the alley," he said, and the corners of his mouth went up a millimeter. "It doesn't get cleaned until midnight. Tide runs toward truth if you know where the drains are."

Naomi wanted to hug him and didn't, because some men love you best when you let them keep their hat on.

They walked Micah home that afternoon and the following afternoon. An angel in front because some animals need to see teeth to understand grammar. Ruth is on the left because mercy guards the soft places better than metal. Naomi was on the right because her presence had become the thesis statement of a town that refused to footnote itself anymore. Tess walked a step behind Micah like a shadow that had decided to be light.

At the corner by the mural, two of the boys pretended not to see them. The third one looked too long and then looked away in a hurry, with an apology stuffed in its pockets. "He's got a grandmother," Ruth said softly. "We'll invite her to the circle."

"Logistics," Angel murmured, and made it sound like poetry.

The page tried to hold Naomi that night and almost failed. She sat at her desk and opened Caleb's notebook to a page she hadn't read because grief had hidden it from her: *If you stand long enough, the ground remembers you. Don't give it up.* She wrote the sentence again in her own hand, slower, and the pen made a groove in the paper like a furrow a farmer trusts to catch water when it rains.

A thought sidled up: *You could go. Sell the house. Start over, where your last name is all that matters.*

She wrote that down, too, because Ruth had told her words lose weapons when they meet ink. *Leave.* Then beneath, the word she'd squared earlier: *Stay.* She added an arrow and the smallest prayer she owned: *Strength.*

Her phone buzzed. A text from Angel: **u eat?** Naomi sent back a picture of a piece of toast shaped like a state that doesn't exist. Angel replied with three knives and a peach.

Ruth sent a photo right after: the women's circle's folding chairs set in a tidy, imperfect oval, one chair featuring a cardigan draped over it like someone promising to come back next week.

Evelyn knocked on the door the way she used to knock to keep words down, but this time the rhythm had changed. "Tea?" she asked, not to calm but to companion.

Naomi closed the notebook and let the word *Stay* glow on the inside of her eyelids as if burned there by a gentle sun.

Millstone's rumor mill tried one more gear before it stripped itself.

"She's cursed," someone whispered near the post office boxes. "The town was fine until she—"

"The town was quiet," Ms. Calloway said, not looking up from her stack of returns. "It wasn't fine."

A flyer appeared on the church bulletin board advertising a "Unity Night," all italic fonts and doves. Someone had drawn a line through *unity* and written *honesty* above it in a child's careful block letters. No one erased it.

At dusk, a car idled at the end of the block longer than a car needs to idle, then pulled away when Angel stepped into the street and scratched her ear with two fingers like boredom had learned to scowl. Motion lights popped on down the row of houses, not because the bulbs had timers but because fear had one and it had gone off early.

Naomi stood on the porch with Evelyn and watched the town choose, not once but again and again, one small choice at a time—the only way towns ever choose for real. The mural across the way captured twilight and transformed it into color. The clay spoon, labeled the Museum of Failed Ideas, sagged slightly in the damp air yet remained legible.

"Breaking point," Naomi said.

"Bending point," Ruth said, coming up the steps with a bag of shortbread like a parable that crunches.

"Point of no return," Angel added, and grinned as if that were the best kind.

Micah lifted a hand from his porch. Tess didn't, but her mouth wasn't a hard line anymore; it was a mouth again, with words it would choose.

Naomi breathed slowly, deep, the way she'd taught her body to in rooms that didn't want oxygen. The inhale reached back to her grandfather's knocks and didn't stop at them. The exhale reached forward to a morning she hadn't seen yet and made space.

"We aren't done," she said. "But we are not what we were."

"Write that down," Ruth said, and Naomi did, on the doorframe with her finger, invisible and permanent.

CHAPTER

21

Grace in the
Grindstone

Sunday pressed itself against Millstone like humidity—every breath work. Hope Chapel filled early, pews polished to a shine that couldn't distract from the grit under everyone's tongues. Naomi slid into the third row with Evelyn, Ruth, and Angel. The church smelled like lilies, lemon oil, and the kind of worry that wears perfume.

Reverend Carter shuffled papers that didn't want to be held. He stepped to the pulpit and gripped its edges as if the wood might remember what to say. "Micah 6:8," he began, voice steady by force. "What does the Lord require of us? Do justice. Love mercy. Walk humbly with your God."

A murmur rolled—some relief, some recoil. He went on: "We've called quiet *peace*. We've called obedience *wisdom*. We've asked the small to make themselves smaller so the big don't have to change shape." He paused. "That is not humility. That is fear dressed up."

Heads turned back toward Naomi. In the second pew, Sister May clutched her hat. Joe, farther down the aisle, shifted like a man sitting on a stone.

Carter tried to land the sermon in the safe field. "Unity matters," he said, then added quickly, "but unity without truth is a choir singing in the wrong key." He closed his Bible. "We will be a church that walks humbly **toward** truth."

The hymn that followed labored through throats that didn't trust themselves. Evelyn sang anyway, her alto clean as a ribbon.

In the narthex, after the benediction, the fracture stepped out from under its Sunday clothes. Sister May took Naomi's hand in both of hers. "Child," she said, voice soft as starch, "you've split this town."

"The crack was there," Naomi answered. "We just stopped carpeting it."

Joe moved close enough to be heard. "LeBlancs bring division," he muttered. "We were fine before."

"Fine and quiet are cousins," Ruth said without looking at him, as if reading a psalm.

Tess flinched at Joe's tone and opened her mouth, then shut it with a swallow that looked like it hurt. Micah's jaw set like a door that didn't plan to swing for the wrong hand anymore.

At home, Evelyn pulled a smaller trunk from beneath the hall table—its brass corners dulled by years of pretending not to exist. She lifted out receipts, letters, notes with her husband's uneven hand.

"Don't," she whispered to herself. Then: "Do." She laid a letter on the table, dated fifteen years back, stamped with Paul's office's tidy logo. *Assistance contingent on continued cooperation.*

Ruth read it slowly. "They called it help," she said. "It was a leash."

Angel leaned over the table. "Your daddy was doing triage," she said gently to Naomi. "Wrong tools. Wrong doctor. Still a man trying to stop a bleed."

Evelyn's mouth trembled. "I told him we had to eat. I said the house comes before the howl. I said we could howl later." She pressed her knuckles to her eyes. "I taught you to hush."

Naomi flattened the paper with her palm. "We survived in a grave," she said. "Now we live." She looked at Evelyn. "We don't pass this down. The chain ends here."

Evelyn nodded once, like a woman taking a vow in a language she'd forgotten she knew.

Angel pulled up a chair beside her, boot against chair leg like a guard dog settling. Ruth set a hand over Evelyn's. The four women formed a small square that the enemy couldn't walk through without learning something about himself.

By late afternoon, the market seethed. Mason's glass door dinged, and Naomi was swallowed into aisles buzzing like bees, deciding whether to sting. Two men squared off near the canned tomatoes.

"She's saving us," one said, big hands open, palms up.

"She's ruining us," the other snapped. "You want your kids blacklisted for scholarships? Speak up like her."

"I want my kids to know the price of their yes," the first answered.

A can toppled. The second man shoved the first. The shove came back with interest. A display of chips collapsed in a rush like paper leaves.

Loretta materialized between them, apron on, eyes sharp. "This isn't a fight," she said. "This is fear trying to find a face it can punch." She jabbed a finger toward the mess. "Pick up your regret off the floor. Both of you."

They did, muttering apologies that sounded like language learning how to crawl. People shifted, embarrassed at their own hands.

Naomi paid with cash and looked the clerk in the eye until his shoulders lowered. At the door, she turned back. "The ledger is older than any of us," she said, not loud, not performative—just pitched to reach the people who wanted to hear. "We can cross out the debt. We don't have to cross out each other."

Outside, two teenage girls stood with bags of flour like shields. One whispered, "Thank you," and blushed when Naomi met her gaze. The other stared, unblinking, curious as a cat who's met its match and is delighted by it.

Night took its time coming, then arrived all at once. On the porch, the clay pot museum of threats glimmered under the light. Naomi sat with

Caleb's notebook open across her knees, pen hovering like a bird unsure of its branch.

"I keep thinking," she said, "what if I broke Millstone?"

"You broke the **spell**," Ruth answered. "Different thing."

Angel blew air through her lips. "If a spell breaks and a town wakes up cranky, that's called morning."

Naomi wrote: *If a thing shatters, maybe it was glass. If it fractures and plants grow through, maybe it was earth.* She set the pen down. "I want earth."

"You have it," Evelyn said from the doorway, blue dress draped on the chair like a flag remembering its pole. "We do, too."

Across the street, Micah lifted a hand. Tess leaned against the rail, chin high, not a dare this time—an introduction to her better self.

Millstone was cracked, yes. The question wasn't whether it would break further. It was whether something honest would rise to the surface.

Naomi breathed deeply enough that her ribs made room for her. The inhale felt like an inheritance reclaimed. The exhale felt like debt forgiven.

CHAPTER
22

*Speak Life
or Be Silent*

———

The post office line curled like a question mark. Naomi stood with bills and a plain manila envelope addressed to herself—a habit she'd started when keeping proof felt safer than keeping peace. Behind her: whispers trying to behave.

"…papers missing…"

"…ledger wasn't *really* locked…"

"…if it comes out, he's finished…"

The clerk stamped her envelopes too hard; each thud landed like a confession. On the way out, two women Naomi had grown up around paused at the door to examine the bulletin board like scholars.

"I told my boys to keep their heads down," said the first. "Kept them safe."

"Kept them small," said the second, then, softer: "I did it, too."

They didn't look at Naomi. She didn't interrupt their learning.

Evelyn set another envelope on the kitchen table that evening, the paper worn soft at the corners. "I was going to burn it," she confessed. "But I don't burn anymore. I bring."

Inside: her husband's notes. Tidy lines in a hand that never looked like it would betray anyone—*extension… favor… speak in your favor if called…* The words felt heavier than the paper deserved.

Tess, arriving with a casserole she swore was "not charity—calories," stopped short at the page. "He did that?" she asked, voice thin.

Evelyn nodded. "We both did, when silence came by with a receipt and a smile."

Micah came in behind her, tool belt slung, sweat at his temples. He read without touching. "I want to be recorded differently," he said. "When the town writes the next page."

Angel whistled low. "You can't choose your ledger. You can choose your line on it."

Ruth spread the notes, the nurse's memos, the ledger copy from the janitor, the summary from Ms. Calloway's archives. Paper made a map. "We're done with rumor," Ruth said. "Truth is written. We'll let the town read."

Naomi slid Caleb's notebook to the corner of the table so it could watch.

The first confrontation occurred at Main and Elm because that was where Millstone liked to pretend it was a movie set. Paul timed his walk to intersect Naomi's, his smile done up like Sunday.

"Miss LeBlanc," he said, each syllable measured to sound like care. "I hear you've been carrying papers that don't belong to you."

"They belong to anyone silence taxed," Naomi answered, pulling the ledger copy from her bag. The paper flashed dull under a cloud. "This is the price list."

A small crowd adjusted its pace to become an audience. Ms. Talley from the market. Mr. Harris from the barber shop. Two kids with bicycles and popcorn that they hadn't bought.

"You're misinterpreting generosity," Paul said. "A town survives on favors."

"A town survives on bread and breath," Naomi said. "Yours ran on debt and hush."

A muscle hopped in his jaw. "This spectacle hurts people," he said. "You'll regret it."

Naomi took one step closer, not aggressive, simply unwilling to be moved by gravity she hadn't agreed to. "We already regret what got us here."

A door opened across the street. Loretta leaned against her frame, wrapped in a dish towel. "If you two are going to rewrite the town charter, do it loud enough for the cheap seats," she called.

Paul's smile flattened. He tipped his head and walked on. Behind him, three men tried to follow, only to remember they had places to be.

He tried again at the council steps two hours later, catching Naomi at the bottom of the stairs. The old courthouse clock didn't ring on the hour anymore, but everyone still looked up at it like it would.

"Miss LeBlanc," he said, quieter, the vowels less polished. "This isn't wise. You're young enough to build a life somewhere else. Don't anchor it to a stunt."

"It isn't a stunt," Naomi said. "It's a ledger with initials."

He reached into his jacket and brought out a folded statement on thick paper—the same she'd refused before. "A path back," he said. "We speak together. We heal."

"We can only heal from what we admit," Naomi answered. She held up her manila folder, the nurse's memos peeking out, the janitor's copies crisp and neat. "Admit."

A councilwoman with a floral scarf walked between them, keys in hand, eyebrows raised. "If you two are going to block the steps, at least file your paperwork," she said dryly, then held the door for Naomi. The door shut on Paul's following sentence and caught it in the hinge.

Inside, the clerk looked up, startled and then relieved. "We have a form for ethics submissions," she said. "We never use it."

"We will now," the councilwoman said, and the clerk found the form in a drawer that stuck before it gave up.

Naomi filled the boxes, initialed the witness line, and slid copies across the counter like communion. When she stepped back into the sunlight, the air felt like a window opened in a room that had been pretending it was outdoors.

Paul stood at the bottom step with his hands in his pockets like a man looking for change and finding none.

By evening, Millstone's rumor mill had eaten enough facts to change its diet. "They filed," someone whispered at the diner. "There's a committee now." "My cousin says there's microfilm." "My aunt says Ms. Oates has a folder thick as a cake." "The nurse kept copies." "The janitor knows which chair hides things."

At the library, Ms. Calloway placed a gray metal box in the glass case, accompanied by a typed card: **Council Ledgers (Extracts), 2001– 2007. Donor Correspondence (Selected).** Underneath, smaller: **Records we almost lost. Courage we won't.**

Kids pressed their noses to the glass and fogged it with breath they didn't bother to apologize for.

That night, Naomi opened Caleb's notebook to a dog-eared page. *If truth costs you everything, at least you won't be bankrupt in the grave.* She copied the line, then wrote beneath it:

Unmasking isn't ripping. It's light. The mask curls at the edges, glue loosens, and the face learns what air tastes like. The town's face is pink and new. It will sting. Then it will feel.

She turned the page and wrote the names that would not be lost—Reed Oates. The nurse whose badge had a first name on it and a last initial she'd learned to own. The janitor who swept courage into piles and left them where people tripped over them. The clerk who found the form. The councilwoman who held the door. Ruth. Angel. Evelyn. Tess. Micah. Caleb. *Me.*

The house creaked, but the sound was a settling, not a warning.

Morning brought fewer whispers and more sentences spoken at full volume. The mask had slipped. Millstone looked at itself in the window of the diner as it passed and didn't flinch as much. Paul walked by the mural without stopping. The town noticed—because the town noticed now.

The unmasking had begun. Nothing would cover it again.

CHAPTER
23

The Unmasking

The council hall had never been this full. Folding chairs scraped against the wood floor, children perched on laps, old men leaned on canes by the door. The rule-man fumbled with his gavel and wiped sweat from his temples. He was accustomed to small gatherings, not an audience that resembled a revival more than a formal procedure.

Naomi sat in the second row, Evelyn at her side, wearing a blue dress. Ruth and Angel anchored her like guardrails—one calm, one sharp. Tess and Micah slid in near the back, their faces pale but set.

Paul entered late, carrying a folder thick with papers. His smile looked polished but tired, a mask that had been worn too long. The whispers followed him like a train of smoke.

The gavel struck. "This is a town council hearing," the ruleman declared, his voice wobbling. "Public comments limited to two minutes."

Angel muttered under her breath, "Two minutes to name a lifetime? We'll see."

Paul claimed the floor first. His voice carried the ease of a man used to being believed.

"Brothers and sisters," he said, palms open. "Our town has been shaken. Rumors have spread, tearing at the fabric of our unity. We must remember that Millstone survives because we trust each other. Division is the true enemy—not the men and women who've sacrificed to keep us standing."

A few heads nodded. But more remained still, arms crossed.

Naomi rose slowly. Her chair scraped, a sound sharper than the gavel. "My name is Naomi LeBlanc," she said, voice steady. "And I will not be silent."

The rule-man stammered. "Ma'am—"

"No," Naomi cut in. "The rule was silence. Silence bought with debts, enforced with fear. That rule is broken."

She held up the ledger copy. "This is not a rumor. This is not gossip. This is the price of obedience—documented, initialed, dated. My father signed. My family carried it. But I refuse to pass it down."

Gasps rippled through the crowd. Evelyn rose beside her, trembling but upright.

"I taught my children to hush," she said. "I wrung rags. I knocked over tables. I told them silence kept us alive. I was wrong. It kept us captive."

Her voice cracked, but she pressed on. "We are done knocking. Done wringing. Done hiding."

Ruth stepped forward next. Her voice was calm, but it reached the corners of the room. "The Lord requires justice, mercy, and humility. Not bargains in shadows. Not hush in the pews. If truth divides, then it divides light from dark."

Angel followed, fire in her eyes. "Peace isn't quiet," she said. "Peace is justice with both hands. They told us unity meant keeping our mouths closed. I say unity means opening them all at once."

Micah surprised everyone by moving forward. His voice shook, but it carried. "I read Caleb's notebook once," he said. "He wrote, *If you can't stand up, sit up. If you can't sit up, speak up. If you can't speak, breathe like you mean it.*" He swallowed. "I'm standing now. I'm not alone."

Tess rose beside him, her face pale but her chin high. "I was afraid the truth would ruin us. But silence already did. If honesty breaks Millstone, let it break honest."

Loretta stood in the back, her apron still dusted with flour. "I'm tired of refilling coffee for cowards. You want pie in my diner, you better order it with your whole voice."

Ms. Oates leaned on her cane, Reed's photo clutched in her other hand. "They took my lights," she said. "But not my boy's name. You don't get to hush me anymore."

The nurse spoke next, badge pinned back on her scrubs. "I lost hours for telling the truth late. But I will not lose my soul for telling it never."

The room erupted—applause, shouts, some cries.

Paul's face tightened. He stepped forward, folder in hand. "These are dangerous lies," he snapped. "Unity matters more than grievances. If you keep this up, you'll tear Millstone apart."

Naomi turned toward him. "Millstone was already torn. You just taught us to cover the rip with silence. We won't anymore."

She lifted the ledger high. "This is the reckoning. No more hidden debts. No more quiet bargains. If unity means obedience, then let it die. We choose truth."

The first clap came from Loretta—loud, deliberate. Angel followed, then Ruth, then Tess. The sound grew until the whole room thundered with it.

Paul tried to speak, but his words drowned under the roar. For the first time in years, his voice was not the loudest.

Evelyn squeezed Naomi's hand. "We're not alone anymore," she whispered.

Naomi lifted her chin, voice carrying above the noise: "My name is Naomi LeBlanc. Caleb's sister. Evelyn's daughter. And I will not be silent."

The gavel struck again and again, desperate to restore order. But order wasn't coming back. Millstone had chosen a different sound.

The reckoning had come.

CHAPTER
24

Storms That Set Free

———

Morning in Millstone didn't arrive quietly; it arrived layered. Radios argued with birds. Screen doors rehearsed their hinges. The neat line between gossip and news blurred like chalk in rain.

Naomi sat on the porch steps with coffee cooling in her hands. Across the street, Micah lifted a hammer with nothing to hammer and set it down as if his muscles needed the ritual of readiness. Tess tied and retied her hair, a metronome for indecision. Evelyn came out in her robe, the blue dress hanging on the chair back like a flag that had learned to be fabric again.

"Do you hear it?" Naomi asked.

Evelyn tilted her head. Debates floated from corners, laughter bubbled from a yard, and two men practiced apologies under their breath, like lines from a play. "I hear living," she said. "Not hiding."

By nine, the corners had become classrooms. At the hardware store, a circle of men stood with paint swatches as if color were philosophy.

"We need unity," the tallest insisted, swatch labeled **Antique White** clutched like scripture.

"We need truth first," the shortest replied, holding **River Stone**. "Let the wall be honest before it's pretty."

Across the street, two teenage girls with backpacks painted over a slur someone had scrawled on a brick column—one brushed **UNITY**, the other **TRUTH** over it in a different hand. They stepped back. Left both. The words overlapped like a Venn diagram.

At the grocery, a daddy shushed a little boy who had asked, loudly, "Was Miss Naomi bad?" His wife touched his wrist. "Don't hush him. Answer him." The man crouched, knees popping. "She told the truth even when it cost. That's what brave is." The boy nodded, filed it, and asked for cereal shaped like stars.

On porches, women washed the steps more than they needed to. In the kitchen, men wiped already clean tables. It's how a town practices doing something when the real work is invisible.

Paul began shrinking where everyone could see it. He walked into the bank lobby with his folder of papers and found a reception desk busy with suddenly intense stapling. The branch manager met him with a pleasant smile, a warmth that was absent.

"Just checking in," Paul said, hand hovering above the counter like a bird uncertain of landing. "We'll move forward with the downtown block once this... fever passes."

"Of course," the manager said with professional kindness, which is to say no. "We'll revisit after the ethics committee completes its review."

Paul nodded as if he'd suggested it. On the way out, he passed a bulletin board where a flyer for the "Unity Night" had been edited by a child's careful block letters again: *HONESTY*. The tape held.

At the lodge—one of those rooms where deals aged like whiskey in the collective memory—he met allies who had mislaid their spines somewhere between Friday and Monday. "We should let this breathe," one ventured. "We are not the enemy," said another, which in Millstone means *we might be losing*. Paul smiled, but the expression sat on his face like a borrowed hat.

He still had a pew at church, but it wasn't the front one anymore. On Sunday he sat in the fifth row with a hymnal open to a song he didn't sing.

Family Fallout required more chairs.

Evelyn called them in the afternoon—Naomi, Ruth, Angel, Tess, Micah, even Bernice, who hovered like a conscience not ready to sit. The blue runner on the table made the room look like it had remembered joy.

Evelyn placed her palms flat. "I taught us the wrong survival," she began. "I made quite a sacrament."

Bernice stared at the runner as if it might tell her how to breathe. "I told my children fear was love," she said at last. "If I fed it enough, it would feed us back. It didn't."

Tess stood, sat, stood again—restless, brave. "I was mad at Naomi because she made Micah brave," she admitted. "Then I realized she just pointed at it. He already had it."

Micah cleared his throat. "I don't want to be a lesson," he said gently. "But if I am, let it be the kind that helps."

Angel reached and squeezed his shoulder. "It is," she said. "And you are."

Ruth slid index cards into the center like bread. On them, three words: **Justice. Mercy. Humility.** "Pick one today," she said. "Practice it for a week. Next week, pick a different one."

Bernice surprised herself by choosing **Humility**. "I'm better at apologies than I thought," she said, cheeks pink. Tess picked **Justice** without asking permission. Micah took **Mercy** and folded the card as if it were a promise.

Evelyn didn't choose. She stood, crossed to the trunk, lifted the old dish rag—the one that had once wrung out fear—and washed it with hot water and soap as if ritual could reverse time. She hung it on the line in full sun. When it dried, she folded it carefully, wrote a note, and placed both in the trunk: *We survived this way. We live this way no more.*

When she closed the lid, nobody clapped. It felt more like a prayer than a performance.

Community Threads braided themselves without waiting for permission.

At Ms. Oates's house, the porch became a parlor for public courage. She set a pitcher of lemonade on a table made from two milk crates and a yard-sale door and didn't say "come in"—people knew. A man from three houses down confessed he'd kept his head down because his father had and his father's father had. "It made sense until it didn't," he said. Ms. Oates nodded and refilled his cup.

A young mother admitted she'd told her daughter, "Don't make waves." "I changed it yesterday," she said. "Now it's 'Learn to swim with your eyes open.'" The porch hummed its approval. A teen boy confessed he'd written *LEAVE* on a paper band around a rock because his cousin dared him. Ms. Oates looked him in the face and said, "Don't be an accessory to someone else's cowardice." He cried, which is a better beginning than swagger.

At the clinic, the nurse returned to find a waiting room fuller than the schedule justified. "We're here for her," a grandfather said, nodding at the badge with her first name and last initial. The manager appeared with a clipboard and six new hours as if he'd invented mercy. The nurse took the hours, then took an extra five minutes between patients to breathe gratitude into her own lungs.

That evening, Loretta hosted a "No Silence Supper" without calling it that. She put long tables together, covered them with butcher paper, and laid out jars of pickles and bowls of potato salad, like a peace treaty with taste. "Eat loud," she instructed. "If you can't be kind, be quiet while you learn," said a new sign in her handwriting over the register. People laughed, then obeyed.

Ms. Calloway installed a glass case at the library's entrance labeled **COMMUNITY ARCHIVE** with a typed card: **Records we almost lost. Courage we won't.** Children pressed their faces to the glass and fogged it with unabashed breath. She didn't wipe it away right away.

The janitor started sweeping the council aisle more slowly, then even more slowly, as if dust remembers what meetings forget.

Naomi's interior weather changed more slowly than the town's.

At her desk, she opened Caleb's notebook and read his lines out loud like liturgy.

If you can't stand up, sit up.
She whispered: "Sitting is still resistance when they want you prone."

If you can't sit up, speak up.
Her pen moved: *Speaking is breath on purpose. It is prayer and defiance in one body.*

If you can't speak, breathe like you mean it.
She wrote slower: *Breath is the first language. I forgot that. The town forgot that. We are learning it again.*

She traced the letters of his name with her fingertip until they warmed under her skin. Then she wrote her own beneath it—not to equal him, but to join him: *Naomi LeBlanc.* The name didn't tremble.

She listed what had changed:

- **Paul** sits in the fifth pew.

- **The ethics committee** has keys to the records room.

- **The nurse** works real hours.

- **Ms. Oates** hosts courage.

- **Loretta** feeds the truth.

- **Ruth** builds circles that hold.

- **Angel** runs logistics that feel like love.

- **Evelyn** put the rag away.

- **Bernice** says, "I was wrong."

- **Tess** shows up.

- **Micah** signs his name to the next page.

- **I** am still here.

She underlined the last one twice.

The ethics committee's first meetings felt like a new language: motions, seconds, votes that mattered. The councilwoman with the floral scarf chaired with a gavel that sounded more like a knitting needle—clicks stitching policy out of the air. The clerk produced forms that no one knew they had. The rule-man, to his credit, listened without interrupting until the habit of interrupting lost muscle tone.

They read the first report in public. It did not grandstand; it did not dramatize. It listed: **irregularities** and **exceptions**, unlogged subsidies, and favoritism tied to "relationships." It recommended audits, open meetings, and the resignation of any official who had "knowingly maintained opacity detrimental to the public trust."

It didn't name Paul outright. It didn't have to. He stepped down from the development board that evening. He left the building by the side door, which is how men leave when they are not being chased but feel like they are.

Reverend Carter changed the marquee himself that night. The letters rattled in the holder as if agreeing. **STILL BREATHING** fits easily. Under it, he added: **BUILT NOT BROKEN**. The wind lifted the words and set them back down.

That night, Naomi walked. Not to be seen; to see.

She passed through porches filled with card games and small, earnest arguments. She heard a teenager say, "I'm sorry, Mama," without sarcasm, and a man say, "I was afraid," without excuse. Two little girls chalked the word **ENOUGH** on the sidewalk and then drew a heart under it, not to soften it, but to finish the sentence.

At the mural behind the post office, the paint had dried into the brick like it was born there. A new hand had added a small **REED** in the lower right corner with a date. Naomi touched the edge of the R and felt gratitude move up her arm like heat from a stove.

She turned toward home. The clay pot "museum" sat on the step, its spoon label slightly crooked from rain. Someone—no one would admit it—had written **THANK YOU** across the top of the rock in chalk. The letters would wash away. The sentiment wouldn't.

Evelyn waited on the porch with two cups of tea. Ruth arrived with shortbread and a verse she didn't read aloud because not every blessing needs a microphone. Angel came with peaches and a look that promised to walk anyone anywhere, anytime.

They sat in the kind of quiet that sounds like safety does when it learns to speak up.

"I thought the aftermath would be silence," Evelyn said. "It's...loud."

"It's living," Ruth corrected gently.

"It's logistics," Angel added, and grinned when Ruth elbowed her.

Naomi opened her journal to a clean page and wrote, not for the committee, not for the town, but for the lungs inside her ribs:

We are not finished. We are not fixed. We are not hiding. We are not hush. We are a people learning to breathe in public again.

She looked up. Across the street, Micah lifted a glass in a toast that needed no words. Tess waved with her chin as if admitting to joy slowly so it wouldn't spook. Bernice opened her door and stood in it without stepping out—tonight, that counted as far as crossing a state line.

The night gathered around them like a quilt pieced from old shirts and new cloth. Porch lights winked on, one by one, like stars that had decided to live local.

Naomi filled her lungs until her body found the room it needed to be in. The air tasted like rain that finally kept its promise.

Aftermath wasn't quiet.

It was **still breathing**—louder, truer, together.

CHAPTER

25

What Remains

The days that followed didn't so much pass as gather. Millstone learned a new sound—voices that did not whisper. Porch swings creaked like metronomes keeping time for conversations that had never been allowed to stretch their legs. The town coughed up its old dust and called it weather, then realized the air felt lighter because something heavy had finally been set down.

Naomi woke early to it all, the town's new music. From the porch, she watched morning pull itself across the street—Bernice sweeping the steps, Micah drinking water from the garden hose like a boy and like a man, Tess tying and retying her hair as if choosing a path with each knot. Evelyn joined her, blue dress hanging on the chair back, a cotton robe replacing armor.

"Do you hear it?" Naomi asked.

Evelyn listened. The wind pushed a screen door, and laughter rolled out with it, unembarrassed. A radio in the distance fought with birdsong and lost on purpose. Someone called out a name from a porch and didn't shush themselves.

"I hear breathing," Evelyn said.

At the diner, Loretta posted a second sign: NO SILENCE SERVED HERE — REFILLS STILL FREE. Coffee flowed, biscuits vanished, and opinions arrived in full sentences. A pair of farmers argued until one of them laughed first; the room joined on instinct, relieved to find out disagreement didn't have to end in exile. Three teenagers sat in a back booth sketching something on brown paper with a golf pencil pilfered from a crossword—lines curling into letters, letters into a phrase they wouldn't show anyone yet.

Ruth slipped through the door with a notebook and a stack of index cards. Angel followed, wearing yesterday's boots and tomorrow's grin.

"Roll call," Angel said, claiming a stool like a throne. "Who needs escorting tonight? Nurse? Ms. Oates? Anyone else who's on a list but doesn't want to be lonely on it?"

Ruth slid one index card to Naomi: Women's Circle—Wednesdays, Fellowship Hall, no microphones, no minutes, no shame. On the back, a verse in Ruth's tidy hand about honest scales and the Lord liking them best.

Naomi thumbed the card, the cardstock warm from Ruth's palm. "You always plan with five loaves and two fish," she said.

Ruth smiled. "Miracles like a little organization."

Loretta set down four plates without asking what they wanted, as if hunger had one menu. "Eat," she commanded. "You can't hold up a town on an empty stomach."

Midday, Ms. Calloway called from the library with a tone that meant, "Come now." When Naomi arrived, the lights were off in the stacks, and the blinds were shut against the afternoon glare. On the main desk sat a grey metal box, locked once, twice, and then forgotten.

"Found it in the donations closet behind a broken globe," Ms. Calloway said, triumphant. "Microfilm reels and a roll of originals. People hide the truth in strange places."

She fed the reel into the machine with the reverence of a sacristan preparing a chalice. Light shone through tiny frames; the pages flashed like fish in a stream. Council Minutes—2004. Grants—2007. Donor Ledgers (Incomplete). In one corner, an old editorial that never made it to print: *We keep confusing quiet with peace. One day, our children will read the silence we taught them like law.*

"Can we copy these?" Naomi asked.

"We can preserve them," Ms. Calloway said, correcting with love. "Copy sounds like theft. What we're doing is saving the record from erasure."

They made three sets—one for the library's new "community archive" box, one sealed for the church safe (Ruth's idea), and one Naomi stuffed into a plain manila folder. Angel walked in halfway through, took two reels and a grin. "I'll store one under my spare tire," she said. "Nobody checks there but me."

By evening, the teenagers' secret at the diner stepped out into the sun. On the brick wall behind the post office—over the faded spray-painted ENOUGH—a cluster of kids from the high school art club set up stepladders. They chalked outlines with lines too confident to be guesses, then rolled paint like they were frosting a cake they had waited all year to eat. People gathered, first in curiosity, then in blessing. Angel guarded the ladders like they were holy relics. Ruth blessed the brushes by handing out bottled water.

The mural bloomed in three layers. First, a backdrop of soft greens and quiet blues—the town's fields and sky, but steadier. Then faces—simple, not portraits so much as invitations: old and young, light and dark, some lined, some smooth. Finally, words, painted by hands that didn't shake: STILL BREATHING.

A boy set down his brush and stepped back. "We wanted it big enough you couldn't pretend not to see it," he said.

Loretta cried openly and didn't call it allergies. Ms. Oates touched the wall with her fingertips and left a smudge like a signature. The nurse stood with her manila folder to her chest and smiled for the first time in public in a long while.

Naomi watched the phrase dry into brick. The town had learned to read itself.

"Looks like a bang to me," Angel said softly, chin lifted at the words as if they saluted back.

Paul did not come to watch the painting. He had his own gathering—men in pressed shirts in the back room of the development office, voices low, confidence frayed. Through the thin wall, a printer whirred and stopped. Paper jam. It felt like a metaphor too lazy to pretend otherwise.

"They're overreacting," one ally insisted.

"Are they?" another asked, and the question hung like humidity in the air.

Paul leaned forward, knuckles steepled. "This is a cycle," he said. "Uproar, remorse, forgetting. We'll let the town tire itself out. Then we offer a statement about unity, and we keep building like we always have."

A younger man across the table—someone whose boy had been benched the season Caleb spoke up—shifted in his chair. "They have copies," he said, the plural landing like a verdict. "Of everything."

Paul's mouth quivered at one corner before memory put it back in place. "People forget," he said. It sounded this time like an inheritance that wouldn't fit the next generation's hands.

When the meeting broke up, three men left by the side door and didn't come back. The printer remained jammed.

The council called an emergency session for "procedural review"—the kind of meeting where nothing is supposed to happen except deciding when the next nothing will happen. People came anyway, filling every chair, standing two deep against the back wall. Naomi sat mid-row with

Evelyn; Ruth and Angel flanked them, never failing to be left and right like wings.

The rule-man cleared his throat. "No public comment," he announced. "We're here to consider... logistics."

"Logistics," Angel murmured, "is coward in a tie."

Ruth's pen moved. Logistics can honor justice. Or avoid it.

A motion was read, then amended, then motioned again until the language had sanded off its own teeth. The room felt like a pot that was on the verge of boiling over. Finally, an older councilwoman with a scarf tied like she meant color said, "We create an independent ethics committee with subpoena power and we give them keys to the record room. Today."

The room didn't cheer. It exhaled. Votes were called. Hands rose, some shaking. Paul's face found the color of unripe fruit.

"Motion carried," the chair said, and the town learned a new word for miracle: procedure used for truth.

After, in the hall, Reverend Carter told Naomi what he should have said the first time and hadn't found courage to. "I'm sorry I waited for the wind to change," he whispered. "I should have been the first to stand."

Naomi didn't absolve him, because absolution is not a thing people hand out like flyers. She nodded and said, "Then stand now," and he did, and that counted.

The threats didn't vanish. They changed shape.

Anonymous notes stopped appearing on rocks and started showing up as unsigned emails filled with cut-and-paste scripture. A tire went flat on Ruth's old sedan, and she changed it with a competence that embarrassed whoever had done it. The nurse received a call stating she wasn't needed, followed by another correction, and finally a third apology, which sounded like it had been reviewed by a lawyer and a conscience in alternating paragraphs.

Angel started a text thread called We Walk Each Other Home and assigned routes like a field marshal. "We fight with eyes open," she told the teenagers, and taught them the difference between being brave and being foolish. She installed motion lights on three porches and helped Micah hang one, forcing him to climb a ladder in front of his own fear and win.

Ruth's Wednesday circle began with five women. By the third week, there were twelve, and by the fifth, chairs had to be borrowed from the children's wing. They did not spill secrets in the first minutes, the way television says people should. They sat. They breathed. They learned silence could be chosen instead of enforced, and the difference made the room holy.

Evelyn attended the first two meetings but did not speak during them. On the third, she put her hands on the table and said, "I taught my children to hush. I'm learning how to repent without drowning." The women did not clap. They nodded, and then the room did the work silence cannot do—it held.

One afternoon, Bernice stood in Naomi's doorway looking like someone who had found an old photograph of herself and didn't know whether to keep it. "He's leaving," she said without preface.

"Paul?" Naomi asked.

"Joe," Bernice said, and the word fell heavier than expected. "He got an offer on a job in the next county. Said he needs a reset. I told him resets happen in hearts, not zip codes. He packed anyway."

Naomi waited for the rest.

Bernice took a breath of air that had filled up her lungs. "I was wrong," she said, throat thick. "I preached fear and called it safety. I don't know how to undo it."

"Don't undo it," Naomi said. "Outgrow it."

Bernice sniffed, wiped at her cheek with the indignation grief borrows from pride. "You sound like Ruth."

"That's a compliment," Naomi said, and Bernice didn't argue.

Evenings returned to the porch like birds that trust the feeder again. Evelyn embroidered a dish towel with nothing on it—no monogram, no message—just blue thread moving in and out of cloth like breath practicing. Naomi wrote at the little table inside the screen door, and when she got stuck, she stepped out and looked at the mural until words returned on their own.

Caleb's notebook lived open on the arm of a chair now, no longer a relic to be hidden, but a reference, a friend. On a page Naomi hadn't read closely, he had scrawled: *If I die, don't make me a saint. Make me a starting gun.* She underlined it twice—not because Caleb needed the emphasis, but because she did.

Micah crossed the street one night with a folded sheet of paper and a pen. "I want to add my name to the ethics complaint," he said. "I know it's not much. But I want the ledger to remember me differently than it recorded my granddad."

Evelyn fetched sweet tea. Ruth arrived with the committee's official form and a clipboard. Angel showed up, despite no one texting her, and leaned against the porch post, smiling like a guard dog who enjoys the company she keeps.

They filled boxes. They wrote sentences that didn't require an apology to stand. Micah signed last and pressed the pen to the table long enough to indent the wood. "So I'll remember where," he said.

On Saturday, the mural got its name. Not all. Not most. Just enough.

Ms. Oates asked the kids to add "REED" in small letters near the lower right, and Floyd, who had painted the outline of the "S," did it gently, like a man touching a scar that no longer belonged to his body. Naomi asked for CALEB across the center in the color of lake water at noon. Tess added a tiny L at the corner—LeBlanc—and then looked at Naomi with a dare that softened into a smile.

Paul walked by after sundown and did not stop. He saw the names and kept his eyes level. The town noticed, and now it's clear why.

The bang came on a Tuesday, not because Tuesdays are magic, but because habit made them holy.

The ethics committee released its first report. It was plain and cruel in the way that only truth told simply as can be. Irregularities in disbursement. Unrecorded "exceptions." Preferential access linked to donations and relationships. It recommended audits, policy changes, and the resignation of any official who had "knowingly participated in the maintenance of opacity detrimental to the public trust."

Paul resigned from the development board that night. He did not resign from the church because churches typically do not accept or require that kind of paperwork. However, he sat in the fifth pew the following Sunday instead of the first, and that said something that country folk understand better than statements.

The committee called for open meetings for the next three months, and people came, not because they loved meetings, but because they had learned to love showing up where truth might need witnesses. The janitor swept the aisle slowly, like a man savoring purpose. The rule-man smiled less and listened more. The woman with the scarf took off her jacket when the work got hard and rolled her sleeves.

Naomi stood at the back during the first open meeting and didn't speak. Ruth did. Angel did. Ms. Oates did, saying Reed's name like a bell. Evelyn did, voice steady, hands at rest. Tess did, unapologetic. Micah did, and when he finished, people clapped before the chair could tell them not to.

On the way out, Reverend Carter stopped at the marquee and changed the letters himself. The clacking felt like repentance. STILL BREATHING fits easily. BUILT NOT BROKEN did, too. The crosswind shifted just then, carrying the sound across Main, where the mural echoed it back in paint.

Naomi walked home in that echo, the town's lungs expanding and contracting in unison for the first time in years. She opened her notebook at the porch table, turned to a blank page, and did not hurry. The lamp warmed the paper. The night held. Evelyn hummed something old and new at once.

We are not finished, Naomi wrote. *We are not fixed. But we are not hiding. We are not hush. We are a people learning how to breathe again in public.*

She set down the pen and stood. Across the way, Micah lifted a hand. Tess leaned on the rail and didn't pretend not to be there. Angel called out, "Lights out, truth in!" like a corny camp counselor, and made three teenagers laugh. Ruth, on her own porch, raised a glass of water as if it were communion.

Naomi filled her lungs slow, deep, and deliberate. The air tasted like the rain that had been promised and finally kept.

Still breathing.

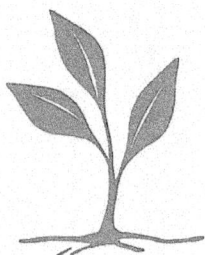

CHAPTER

26

Built Not Broken

Six months later, Millstone walked with a new cadence. It hadn't learned to sprint; it had learned to **stride**. The cracks were still visible, but they looked less like wounds and more like seams where something durable had been stitched.

The mural behind the post office had been touched up three times by the high school art club. The blue of **CALEB** at the center held sunlight like a bowl; along the bottom, smaller names had bloomed— **REED**, the nurse's full name, Ms. Oates in careful block letters, the janitor's first name written in chalk that kept getting traced over by strangers who refused to let it fade. Someone had added tiny lungs in the corner, with the caption 'still breathing'. Children left handprints near the base, a row of small blessings that washed away in the rain and returned by noon the next day.

The ethics committee posted summaries on a corkboard in the town hall lobby: **Findings. Remediations. Next Steps.** No dramatics. Just the plain work of righting. A calendar beside it listed the dates of open meetings. People circled them with pens and brought cookies, just like they were at choir practice.

Loretta's "No Silence Supper" had become a **Thursday** thing. Long tables. Butcher paper. Questions written in marker down the center: *What did you fear? What are you building now?* The answers appeared in different hands—some careful, some messy, some spelled like courage learning phonics. If anyone cried, Loretta topped off their tea and didn't narrate it.

Ruth's Wednesday Circle outgrew the fellowship hall and spilled onto the lawn whenever the weather allowed. The sign read: **No microphones. No minutes. No shame.** On the fifth week of summer, a group of men asked if they could start something similar. "Yes," Ruth said, handing them a box of folding chairs and a stack of index cards labeled **Justice. Mercy. Humility.** "Same rules. Same courage."

Angel ran **Walk Each Other Home** like a dispatch that ran on prayer and group texts. She posted routes, checked on porch lights, taught half the teenagers in town to change a tire, and the other half to apologize with their whole faces. Her jokes had become a kind of safety: "Eyes open. Mouth open only as needed," she'd say, and kids mimicked her cadence like a creed.

At the clinic, the nurse's badge had acquired two stickers from kids and a nameplate from the manager that finally spelled her last name right. "We're doing intake differently now," the manager said one morning, and he meant *better*. Parents asked for her by name. She never let the badge feel light again.

Ms. Oates kept a pitcher on her porch and a chair that matched no other chair on earth. Neighbors stopped by to say things people used to write down and hide: "I didn't speak because I thought I would break," "I didn't speak because I liked being liked," "I didn't speak because I didn't know how." Ms. Oates listened the way elders listen when they know the words are heavier than the mouths carrying them. Sometimes she answered. Sometimes she pressed a photo of Reed into a palm and said, "Say his name out loud." They did, and found it did not crack their teeth.

Evelyn put the rag away and never reached for it again. On afternoons when the light slanted through the kitchen just right, she stitched table runners in the color of forgiveness—blues that matched her dress, threads that caught at the edges like grace does. She wrote a note on the inside cover of the trunk for anyone who might someday find it: *We survived this way. We live this way no more.* The trunk closed without ceremony and stayed shut.

Bernice joined the Wednesday Circle every week she could. She was not the quickest to speak, but when she did, it sounded like floorboards settling after a heavy storm. "I confused fear with love," she said once, and the admission unclenched her mouth for a dozen new sentences. She laughed more easily now, sometimes at herself, sometimes with

Tess, who recorded those laughs in her memory like music she wanted to play back later.

Tess volunteered at the library's **Community Archive**, labeling boxes and teaching kids how to feed microfilm into the viewer without bending the edges. She kept a roll of painter's tape on her wrist and used it like punctuation. "We're not hiding this," she told a middle-schooler who asked why the case was at the front instead of the basement. "We're **saving** it." On Saturdays, she wiped down the mural's lower bricks with a rag and challenged any kid within earshot to draw something that made an old man smile. They did. It worked.

Micah mentored teens on Ruth's porch under a string of lights someone had installed crooked and never corrected. He organized **college nights**, resume Sundays, and a quiet hour, which turned out not to be quiet at all because the kids had questions and Micah wanted them to ask. He signed his name to petitions like a man whose signature meant something to himself, then showed three boys how to do the same. He still carried a hammer sometimes with nothing to build except himself. That was plenty.

Paul nodded when he passed Naomi on Main now. No speeches. No smile too wide. Just a nod. The town nodded back—some with forgiveness, some with neutrality, some with the kind of boundaries that are neither cruel nor flexible. He still had a pew at church. It remained the fifth, and his singing knew when to enter and when to rest. A few people admitted to fearing him more than they let on. Most did not miss it at all.

And Naomi wrote.

Not speeches. Not indictments. **Pages**. Morning pages on the porch with the coffee cooling, evening pages at the small table behind the screen where bugs tapped the mesh like ideas asking admittance. She wrote about breath as the first language. She wrote about Ruth's trinity—justice, mercy, humility—and how it refused to behave unless all three showed up. She wrote about Angel's logistics in a way that felt like love. About Evelyn's repentance that didn't perform. About Loretta's commandments in marker. About the nurse's badge with two stickers. About Ms. Calloway's placard that said, 'Please fog the glass.' About Ms. Oates's pitcher and chair. About Micah's hammer. About Tess's painter's tape. About Bernice's laughter like floorboards. About Caleb's blue name that still held noon.

Some days, she wrote as if the town were a body undergoing physiotherapy: stretching what had atrophied, strengthening what had compensated for too long. Some days she wrote as if the town were a choir relearning harmony after years of humming. Most days she wrote to remind herself that **still breathing** was not the end of a sentence but a clause that lets another begin.

Reverend Carter asked if she would read one page on a Sunday not marked by anything except the burden of the ordinary. She said yes. She stood at the lectern and read about *breath as prayer*, about *confession without spectacle*, about *building with small, stubborn yeses*. When she finished, two teenagers clapped on the wrong beat, and no one corrected them. It sounded right.

The ethics committee released its **final initial report** (a phrase the chair insisted on, to remind everyone that integrity never ends). It outlined what had been mended and what remained. It included a list of standing practices and a reminder: **All records are open by default.** Naomi pinned a copy on the corkboard at the diner. Someone underlined that sentence twice.

One late summer evening, Naomi walked the block alone first to see if she could, then because she wanted to. The mural breathed under the streetlight. The porch lights blinked on in a relay race of domestic constellations. A kid rode a bike with a light fixed to the handlebars that made a circle on the pavement like a moving target he refused to step out of. A couple argued gently and didn't lower their voices; a woman sang off-key while watering impatiens and looked happy to be bad at something public.

She climbed her steps and found Ruth already there with a tin of shortbread and a schedule she pretended not to have written. Angel appeared next with a bag of peaches and a grin that gave away future trouble in benign doses. Evelyn followed with a pitcher of tea and glasses that, despite not matching, belonged together.

"Roll call," Angel said. "Brave? Present. Hungry? Present."

"Mercy?" Ruth asked, eyes warm.

"Present," Naomi answered.

Tess crossed the street with paint under her fingernails and sat on the top step like it was an assigned seat she'd finally decided she liked. Micah brought a stack of flyers about college night and pretended to need Naomi's table to sort them. Bernice lingered at the bottom, then climbed two steps, then three, then sat. The porch made room by becoming bigger without moving.

They didn't say much at first. Breathing counted as conversation.

Angel broke it with a nudge to Naomi's shin. "Two-minute sermon," she ordered, one eyebrow raised. "Timer's imaginary."

Naomi laughed. "No sermon," she said, then stood anyway. She looked out at what existed now: a town that didn't whisper when it meant to talk. A church that had learned to do minutes like they mattered. A diner with commandments in Sharpie. A clinic with a badge that had a name and stickers. A library that asked children to fog the glass on purpose. A mural that told the truth so big even the liars had to read it.

"We were told to hush," she said finally, voice steady enough to cross the street. "We learned to speak. We were told to bow. We learned to stand. We were told we were broken." She paused, hand on the porch rail like a podium built by family. "But we are **built**."

Ruth's hand found hers, simple and sure. Angel leaned her shoulder into Naomi's like teammates after a game whose score they knew without a board. Evelyn breathed out the kind of breath that doesn't apologize for taking up space.

Across the way, Micah lifted a glass in a toast that didn't need words. Tess looked like a girl and a woman at once and let herself smile with both. Bernice put her palm flat on the porch and felt it hold.

Naomi filled her lungs until her ribs gave her more room, then let the air go—slow, deliberate, like signing a document only she could see.

"Built," she said, and the porch wood didn't creak in protest. "Not broken."

The town answered without arranging itself: porch lights like stars, laughter like liturgy, the distant clack of the church marquee letters being rearranged for the week ahead, the soft swish of a broom in the fellowship hall where someone made ready for chairs that would hold tomorrow's stories.

Naomi didn't say *amen*. The night said it for her.

Breathe in. Breathe out.

Built. Not broken. Still breathing.

ACKNOWLEDGEMENTS

This book could not have come to life without the steady love and encouragement of people who reminded me that stories matter—even when they are heavy, even when they hurt.

To my family: thank you for shaping my love for words and for teaching me, in both quiet and loud ways, the weight of truth.

To my friends and mentors who believed in this project when it was only scattered notes and half-formed ideas—your encouragement carried me through every draft.

To the readers who pick up *Built Not Broken*: thank you for giving this story your time, your attention, and your heart. I hope you find pieces of yourself in Naomi's courage and in Millstone's reckoning.

And most of all, to God who gave me the words when I thought I had none—thank You. Every page belongs to You first.

Rachel Gaines

A NOTE TO THE READER

If this book has spoken to you, I invite you to carry its message forward. Share it with a friend who needs encouragement, reread the passages that call you back, and let the story remind you: silence doesn't have the final word.

This is not the end. This is only the beginning of your journey.

Stay connected for future works from both Rachel Gaines and my pen name, M.Y.T. Morrow—including a companion journal designed to give you more space for reflection, prayer, and writing your own story of resilience.

Rachel Gaines

FOR BOOK CLUBS & READERS

Naomi's journey through Millstone raises questions about silence, family, and courage. Use these prompts to spark reflection or group discussion, leaving space for your own thoughts along the way.

Family and Silence
Naomi struggles against a family tradition of silence. Have you ever experienced silence being used as a form of protection—or as a means of control—in your own life or community?

Generational Patterns
The story highlights generational secrets and cycles. Which moments in the book show how the past shaped Naomi's present choices? Do you think generational cycles can truly be broken?

Naomi and Caleb
Caleb's memory hovers over the story. In what ways does Naomi continue his fight, and in what ways does she carve her own path?

The Role of Community
Millstone often feels like a character itself—sometimes suffocating, sometimes protective. How do small-town dynamics (gossip, loyalty, church influence) shape Naomi's struggle?

Faith and Courage
Several characters—Naomi, Evelyn, Ruth, and Angel—interpret faith differently. Which perspective resonated with you most, and why?

Breaking Points
Evelyn's breakdown becomes a turning point for Naomi. What do you think it takes for someone to finally change after years of silence?

Truth vs. Safety
Speaking the truth puts Naomi in danger. Do you think telling the truth is always worth the cost? Why or why not?

The Reckoning
The novel closes with confrontation and transformation. If you were Naomi, would you have made the same choices at the end? Why?

ABOUT THE AUTHOR

Rachel Gaines is a writer, advocate, and speaker dedicated to empowering women to heal, rise, and reclaim their voices. Known also by her pen name, M.Y.T. Morrow, she blends faith, storytelling, and emotional honesty to illuminate the fractures, resilience, and quiet strength that shape the lives of ordinary women.

Her work explores themes of generational wounds, small-town secrets, spiritual growth, and the unspoken battles women carry in silence. Through both nonfiction reflection and spiritually resonant fiction, Rachel creates space for readers to confront truth, embrace healing, and rediscover the courage within themselves.

When she's not writing, Rachel is dreaming up future projects, journaling her own reflections, and encouraging others to honor their becoming. Built Not Broken is the first in a series of works that speak to the power of truth, courage, and grace in the face of silence—offered under both her given name and her creative identity, M.Y.T. Morrow.

Rachel Gaines

COMING SOON

Stay tuned for the next release from M.Y.T. Morrow, a companion novel that continues exploring the threads of family, silence, and resilience woven throughout *Built Not Broken*.

Also on the horizon is a guided journal companion, created to give readers space for reflection, prayer, and writing their own story of courage, faith, and truth.

For those seeking ongoing inspiration, look for *Move. Yield. Transform*, the first book in Morrow's inspirational series. This collection of devotional reflections offers practical wisdom, heartfelt prayers, and intentional pauses to support you on your journey of becoming.

Whether writing as Rachel Gaines or under her pen name M.Y.T. Morrow, each forthcoming work is crafted with the same heart: to help women heal, rise, and reclaim the power of their own story.

CONTACT INFORMATION

M.Y.T. Morrow would love to stay connected with you.

✉@ Email: **author@mytmorrow.com**
✉@ Alternate: **mytmorrowbooks@gmail.com**
▯ Instagram: **@MYTMorrow**

For updates on future releases and resources, follow along and share your own journey of courage and transformation.

www.ingramcontent.com/pod-product-compliance
Lightning Source LLC
LaVergne TN
LVHW091249080426
835510LV00007B/184